My Band of
MERRY MEN
AND JACK BERRY

My Band of
MERRY MEN
AND JACK BERRY
Alan McHardy

PUBLISHING

First Published in Great Britain in 2019 by DB Publishing,
an imprint of JMD Media Ltd

ISBN 9781780915968

Printed and bound in the UK

CHAPTER ONE

AS a young boy I wanted to be one of two things, a vet or a journalist. I had the education to be either, but neither came to be. I did, however, have three collies in my life, each one truly wonderful, and I did train, in most cases successfully, over 100 greyhounds. Instead of my original ambitions I became a clerk, soldier, milkman, driver and sales representative before branching out on my own. I have been lucky enough to have some of the greatest friends any man could wish for. Some of these friends include some of the biggest names in the football and horse-racing worlds. I have been involved in dealings with the dictator Idi Amin and been involved in the investigation into the Yorkshire Ripper. I was also due to meet the Army Payroll Killer Andy Walker the night he was arrested. This book is dedicated to those good friends and relatives who have often suggested I write a book, so read on and who knows someone may actually enjoy reading it.

They always start I was born, and so I was, on 4 June 1943 in the Simpson Memorial Pavilion in Edinburgh. My first 18 years were spent in the historic village of South Queensferry, about which books have been written, and rightly so because it is steeped in history. Sitting on the Firth of Forth, its first claim to fame is the Forth Bridge, the fifth wonder of the world. Under the Bridge sits the Hawes Inn, made famous in Robert Louis Stevenson's Kidnapped. Further along the promenade sits the

Seals Craig Hotel, whose lounge commands a stunning view of the bridge. Towering above the hotel is a large white house called Catherine Bank, and that is where my first 18 years were spent. I mention this because when you look at good/bad and lucky/unlucky things in life, Catherine Bank comes into both good and lucky. Good because the views from our windows were like no other in Scotland. From our two front rooms you could look right and see the entire railway bridge, look left and see the new road bridge from its first bolt to its last. From the centre of the two rooms you had a magnificent panoramic view of both bridges, the river between, Rosyth Dockyard on the far banks of the Forth and the hills of Fife beyond. In fact, postcard companies used to visit the house and take photos for their postcards from our garden, middle rooms and attic. I don't know what, if anything, my family received for these favours, but years on when I was a salesman in my own right I would have made a bob or two for sure.

That was also the time for my first collie, Nell. In those days the evil predators who prey on children never existed in places like Queensferry, and just as well because from the day I took my first steps Nell never left my side. When I went to school she came with me, when I came out at dinner time she was waiting and when school finished she was at the school gates. I was eight when she died and it was the first time my heart was ever broken.

There wasn't a lot going on in the Ferry in those days, one picture house, two cafes, and two fish and chip shops, but we always found plenty to do. Going back and forward on the ferry boats, which unless you did a two-hour diversion via the Kincardine Bridge were the only way across the Forth between North and South Queensferry. Rail travellers on the Forth Bridge considered it lucky to throw coins over, and we revelled in collecting them at low tide. I have seen me get as much as £1, and in the 1940s a pound was nearly a fortune. In the rocks we used to catch crabs and lobsters, which we sold to the local fishmonger. We were also known to do the odd bit of poaching on the surrounding estates owned by Lord Roseberry and the Marquis of Linlithgow, our elders indulged even more and let's say many a home in the Ferry frequently dined on rabbit, pheasant or wood pigeon.

Obviously, I was a wartime baby, and Rosyth on the north side and Lochinvar on our side were hives of activity for the Home Fleet. The Hood sailed from Rosyth for her ill-fated clash with the Bismarck. The Bismarck was sighted, Hood was in Rosyth under repairs but was rushed out with many of the civilian workers still aboard. As history tells us she received a direct hit on one of her magazines and went down, leaving few survivors. My uncles tell me the Luftwaffe made frequent raids on the dockyards, although not nearly as often as Clydebank and nowhere near as deadly. They didn't do much damage to our side of the country as there were warships by the score in the Forth and air bases at Pitreavie, Leuchars, Turnhouse, and Drem so we were well protected.

Until I was 12 it was pretty much village life, but as I mentioned earlier I had some brilliant friends and we remain so to this day, and we could always find some mischief to get up to. We were a mixed lot, the village kids and the farmers' sons and daughters from the neighbouring farms, but did we form lifelong bonds. When I say it was pretty much village life, I did get hit with one traumatic experience. My mother and father divorced; I wanted to stay with my mother, and as giving custody to the mother with arranged access for the father was a mere formality, everything seemed OK. As my father had moved back to his home village of Ushaw Moor in County Durham, his access was agreed to two weeks during school holidays.

We had an elderly friend of my grandfather's called Johnnie Walker who lived with us. Before I go any further I must mention Johnnie was the kindest, most loved man I have ever known. He came on the scene before I was born but the story goes his parents had died, he had nowhere to go, my grandfather brought him home and he was one of the family till the day he died. Everyone in the Ferry loved Johnnie, and it was a sad day when he finally passed away.

Anyway, on the day my father was to pick me up at Dalmeny station, Johnnie dutifully took me to meet him. We were on the train from Edinburgh to what I thought was Durham when the bombshell dropped and my father told me I wasn't coming back, I was staying with him. We didn't go to Durham but instead we went to Bristol where six weeks of hell began. As you will hear later in the story, I was a better-than-average footballer and athlete, so was more than good enough to hold my own anywhere. In the school I was sent to instead of being welcomed into their teams they seemed to resent me. Now in

Queensferry, as I said, we were a great crowd and bullying was unheard of. I got my first taste in Bristol, but luckily I was always strong willed and, though a day didn't go by that I didn't have to fight my corner, they soon got the message and I was left to my own means, which suited me. Lady Luck was looking out for me though, as my father's kindly landlady realised things were not right and slowly won my trust. When I told her the chain of events she contacted my mother and arrangements were made to get me back home. I don't know if my father had a crystal ball, but he suddenly announced we were going to live in Ushaw Moor. Mrs Mills the landlady, however, slipped me enough money to make as many phone calls as was necessary to get my recovery in motion.

We got to Ushaw Moor and I went to school straight away; what a difference, it was like being back in Queensferry. Everyone was friendly – Do you play football? What position? Do you like pigeons (everyone in the village had a loft)? Everywhere I've been in life I have met and liked Geordies, and I am sure that was where it started. Anyway, within a couple of weeks arrangements were made and my Uncle Cyril, a Commando Sgt Major, collected me at Durham bus station and I was on my way home. One last scare, though, was my father was a bus conductor and I had to gamble that the bus I caught from Ushaw Moor to Durham wasn't his.

I was back with my pals, loved it and showed it, as did they. The access rights were reviewed in court, as were my father's actions, and he was still to be allowed access (if I wanted) during the holidays. I wasn't sure at first, but eventually agreed after my uncle warned him of the consequences if he ever tried that trick again. The only real adverse thing to come out of it all was the fact my summer school holidays wouldn't be the same again. I would spend two weeks at Ushaw Moor and two to three weeks with my mother and her partner, who I will mention shortly, in Portsmouth. There was an upside to this. My cousin Penny, a real tomboy, was a keen Portsmouth fan and we used to go to the games. We were always close as kids, and although when we left school and the Portsmouth trips ended, we always kept in touch and Penny is probably my favourite cousin. Anyway, getting back to the games, somehow when I was on holiday it coincided with games against Blackpool and Preston and I was able to marvel at the skills of Tom Finney, Stanley Matthews and the Pompey skipper Jimmy Dickinson. Funnily enough, when I was at Ushaw Moor Newcastle United seemed to catch these two teams, and again, as well as Matthews and Finney, Newcastle had Jackie Milburn and their captain, a Scot called Jimmy Scoular. Some players these guys. The only adverse side was that I didn't spend much of my summer holidays with my Queensferry pals.

It was 12 years before my life started in earnest. The dreaded 11 Plus, or Qualifying exams as we called them, were on us and this was where the Ferry's finest kids came to the stage and we found out if we were brainy, stupid or saveable. We had two main categories, the really brainy went to Bo'ness Academy, the average stayed at Queensferry, as did the stupid, who went into what was called the modifying class. This was where most of the farmers' sons and daughters ended up. They did basic lessons but mainly the boys dug and tended the school gardens and the girls did sewing and knitting. Me? My mother had better plans in mind. By this time, she had moved in with a man who was to be her love for the rest of her life, Alex Herd.

He was a fine man of some wealth and was a senior executive with the gas board. It was decided I was going to George Heriot's, Scotland's leading school. Prince Charles might say Gordonstoun, Tony Blair might say Fettes, Chris Hoy may say Watson's, forget it lads you will never beat or better Heriot's. My only worry was my pals might turn against me, not in a million years as it turned out. Plenty of piss taking, like don't get your new uniform dirty, remember to speak posh, watch your back in the toilets etc, maybe a wee bit of jealousy but genuinely nothing but 'good luck' and 'wish it was me'.

Heriot's was a revelation and the doors it would open in later life were unbelievable but you still had to prove yourself. Just before I started we had some famous former pupils to try and emulate. Kenny Scotland was school captain the year I started and went on to become one of Scotland's all-time greatest full-backs. He was followed by Andy Irvine, another full-back. We had George Goddard and Hamish Moore both capped for Scotland at rugby and cricket. We had numerous other Scotland caps and almost every one of the FP side played intercity.

We had Gerald Dott, probably the world's leading brain surgeon. Every one of my class was talented either at rugby, cricket or athletics. One of our school mates was the boy actor

Paul Young, who later became a well-established actor. The film Geordie had been made starring Bill Travers. Paul played Geordie, a boy in the film, and it was a big hit. The whole school got free tickets for the premiere in the ABC on Lothian Road and we got to meet all the cast. A real experience. You name it, Heriot's produced it. International rugby stars, athletes, cricketers, surgeons, scientists, doctors, lawyers (and a few clients for the said lawyers, myself included). I am truly thankful to my mother and her partner Alex for giving me the opportunity, even though I didn't make the best of it.

We were a rough lot for a fee-paying school, though. A couple of the real rough diamonds once made what they thought were harmless bombs in the chemistry class. They put them on the tram lines and blew the arse out of a tram car. Fortunately, no one was hurt and though we all knew the culprits no one was shopping them.

None of us liked music class and the music master, Mr Halliday, who we called Doc, was a nasty sadistic bastard. On a Saturday in 1956 our beloved Hearts (the entire class were Hearts fans) drew with Raith Rovers in the Scottish Cup semi-final. There were no floodlights in those days so the game was replayed at Easter Road on the Wednesday at 3pm. Our last class that day was music and finished at 3pm. Any other master would have let us away early, but not Doc. We thought about one or two missing class and the rest covering for them, but then bugger it every one of us wanted to be at the game so we stuck together, skipped the class and went. It was worth the hell we got next day from the headmaster and our parents because the Jam Tarts won and went on to win the Cup, beating Celtic 3-1.

Our hero at that time was the driving force behind Hearts, only four or five years older than us. His name was Dave Mackay, and little did I realise then that one day in the future I would become one of Dave's best pals. More about that later though.

Heriot's was a rugby playing school but most of my class were football daft. As a result, we had to find amateur clubs to play football with, but unfortunately when selected to play for the school rugby team you couldn't refuse. Thankfully, school rugby was on a Saturday morning and those of us with football clubs could get away in the afternoon. In those days you could run forever so it was no problem. One lad a class below me made it to the senior level of football: Alan Gordon, who starred for Hearts and almost got the goal that would have won us the title instead of Kilmarnock on the last day of the 1962 season. They say lightning never strikes twice, but it did for Hearts when they again lost the league on goal difference in a 2-0 defeat at Dens Park (more about that later too, as I had more than a vested interest in the outcome).

As you will be aware, my pals and I are getting older, we are starting to realise that girls are not just for having their pigtails pulled, and someone figured a punt on the horses was a good way of increasing your pocket money. Fags appeared, William Younger's screwtops seemed tastier than coffee or juice. Powderhall greyhound track was added to Tynecastle for our sporting visits. Ten miles up the road from

Queensferry was a place called Oatridge and it so happened Linlithgow and Stirlingshire Hunt held their annual point-to-point race meeting there, and, as all our farmer pals' fathers had or knew someone with a horse running there, that was added to our repertoire. Here I am not yet 15 going to the best school in Scotland with pals who right now are the most mischievous mob imaginable, who are going on to become top lawyers, doctors, accountants etc. Anyone assessing us would think God help the country, and that was daytime. Back home after school it was all about my Ferry pals, and though the Ferry wasn't Edinburgh with regards to things to do, we didn't realise that within a year events were going to occur that would bind us for life.

I could have and should have stayed on at school, taken my Highers and gone to university. I was brilliant at English, and with my memory for dates and figures I was the pride and joy of my History master ,who was a real tough war hero of the Long Range Desert Group. Passable at Latin and Geography, good at Natural Sciences, great with figures but useless, stupid, and unsaveable at Geometry, Algebra, Chemistry and Woodwork (and that was the kindest words the masters of these subjects were allowed to use). I didn't go on, I left at 15 and went to work as a clerk, but boy was that a mistake, one thing was for sure it was not what I was cut out for. I did last two years in the Stock Exchange, but that was as an assistant dealer in the exchange itself. I just was not cut out for an office.

Queensferry had no shortage of talented young football players, but we had not had a local team for years. Now, I am not blowing my own trumpet here, but the reason I am writing this book is because my pals (including Dave Mackay) have always urged me to and I was always a sort of ring leader, especially when it was 'I dare you' or any mischievous escapades, so I decided to form an under-16 team and apply to join the Edinburgh under-16 league. Easy said, harder done. Queensferry is only ten miles from Edinburgh, but the buses then only ran every hour. Very few people had telephones. When we arrived in Edinburgh we would then have to take local buses to the various districts where our opponents played, and remember we are country boys who don't know A from B in the city. We have no money, no ground, no changing rooms, no strips. But I eventually got everyone together and outlined what I was doing, and everyone wanted to be in on our adventure. Next step was to contact the league secretary and find out if we would be accepted. He didn't see any problems, but we would have to attend the next monthly meeting, the last one, for us to be accepted for the coming season. My lifelong friend Jock MacDonald and I attended the meeting. Let me explain, though, Jock stayed on a pig farm outside Queensferry and had to walk half a mile to the nearest bus stop. I would join that bus when it passed through Queensferry, so a journey that today would take 20 minutes then was an hour. When we reached the meeting place imagine the incredulous looks on the faces of the adults when two 15-year-old boys turned up asking to join their league. Our enthusiasm must have won the day because we were accepted as Queensferry United, even though we didn't have the £3 required for our registration fee.

We had ten weeks to get organised before our first game and not a pot to piss in. Firstly, I went to the Lord Provost's house and asked him for the use of the only pitch in Queensferry, the Burgess Park, unlined and deeply rutted through, being used by Codona's funfair on the annual fair week. There were other pitches used by the Navy and the Catholic school, but they were unavailable either because we couldn't afford them or they were not being made available to us. Problem one solved, we sorted out the ruts and lined Burgess Park ourselves. I organised a raffle round the pubs and houses and we raised enough to buy our first kit, an all-white set that we bought from the Army and Navy Surplus Stores. We were halfway there. I approached the Church of Scotland minister for use of the church hall for training, which he agreed to. The British Legion Club was halfway up a steep hill called The Loan and 300 yards from the pitch, but it was the nearest we could get so I asked the president for permission to use the club for changing facilities and again permission was granted. We were up and running but still had no funds as such and the match referees had to be paid. After our first training session I explained the situation to the lads and, brilliant as they always were, we started to work things out. For the first few weeks we would have to chip in equally to pay the referee, and we would also pay our fares to the away games. To fund raise every player would sell two raffle books per week. We would run a dance every Saturday night in the local Priory Hut, as it was called, and as soon as possible all out-of-pocket expenses would be returned.

Everything worked as planned. We sold our raffle books, we had full houses at our dances, the pubs advertised our fixtures and when the season started we had between 100 and 150 spectators, and we always had a raffle. The British Legion supplied oranges and tea at half time, support in the village grew, we were home and hosed. But now let me tell you the sacrifices some of these boys had to make and you will understand the bond that was formed. The local lads had only minutes to walk to training, which was every Thursday night. The country lads were strung out on the farms along the Bo'ness road, though, with the exception of Jock MacDonald's half-mile walk, the bus more or less stopped at their farms. It was time consuming because their fathers still expected them to complete their shift on the farm. It was even more difficult for Jock because his father was tragically killed in a car accident returning from a Hearts game at Aberdeen. Jock was the man of the house so his work rate far exceeded that of the other country lads, but he never complained. The unbreakable bond that Jock and I formed for life came one Saturday morning before a home game when we had to line the pitch. In those days you didn't have the paint roller they have now, you did it by hand with sawdust, which the local distillery kindly supplied us with free of charge. We were all supposed to turn up and muck in, though I didn't expect the country lads as they were further away and had their farm work before they could get away to play, but Jock always turned up. This Saturday only Jock and I turned up, so imagine two 15-year-olds carting barrowloads of sawdust up a steep hill, the time-consuming, back-breaking job of lining the pitch then playing a league game. Had the whole squad turned up it would have been a doddle. That afternoon was the only time I laid into the team, and I made it clear that if it ever happened again I would cancel the game and forfeit the points. Since they had elected me team captain, I assured them I wouldn't hesitate. It never happened again.

The season itself? Considering we were playing the cream of Edinburgh talent we did well. Only the five established clubs beat us, and we beat the other six. The favourites won all the cups, but there was a consolation cup for the other sides which we should have won but didn't. We had a year we will never forget, and neither will the village. We didn't play under-17 for various reasons, but as you will hear later we were all to play again later in our lives or come together in other ways.

I was blessed with some fantastic relatives. My grandfather on my mother's side was crippled with World War One wounds, but there was nothing he didn't know about football and my grandmother spoiled me rotten. When they died it was the second heartbreak of my life. My grandfather, who drove me relentlessly to be a decent footballer, did get some reward when I played in the West Lothian Boy Scouts five-a-sides. There were 64 teams involved and my side won it, though it wasn't Queensferry; we were knocked out in the first round. Uphall had two players injured and only one reserve with them, so they asked permission to recruit a player from one of the beaten sides; it was granted, I was approached and went on to win my first-ever trophy, to my grandfather's great delight.

My other grandfather on my father's side was a legend in his time. A miner all his life but a leading trade unionist (I never had any time for politics, have never voted and never will), my grandfather was big time in the Labour Party and I am told he taught Harold Wilson all he knew. Every year (at least in those days) you had the Durham Miners' Gala Day, where from as early as 6am miners led by their band came from all over the county and country. It was a fantastic spectacle, all the banners and bands. My grandfather's picture was the centrepiece of the Ushaw Moor banner and that banner still sits proudly in the Beamish Museum. Like virtually every adult in Ushaw Moor my granddad kept pigeons. He twice won the pigeon derby, the Rennes Race, not just local or country wide but nationally. I still have his first medal and the winning pigeon's rubber ring, which goes in the clock when the bird returns.

I had two aunts who spoiled me rotten: Jean, who married a Canadian and emigrated to Canada, and Mary, who was an absolute gem of a lady and always took my side in any disputes with my parents. Mary married Cyril Pauley, who I respected more than probably any other man alive, with the possible exception of my other uncle, Jimmy McHardy. Cyril was a Marine Commando Sgt Major who landed on Sword Beach on D Day with Lord Lovat. In fact, in the film The Longest Day Lord Lovat leaps off the ramp followed by Sean Connery and Norman Rossington, who played the roles of Cyril and his pal Ginger. He later fought terrorists in Africa and he revelled in showing his first son, my cousin Ian, and I a photo of him and Ginger both holding their trophies, severed terrorists' heads.

He also had photos of his lads playing football with the same heads. My Aunt Mary abhorred violence of any kind and she fairly laid into Cyril when he brought his mementoes out. Ian and I loved it. My other Uncle Jimmy McHardy was also a career soldier and served in Palestine during the conflicts there. He married a Yorkshire girl, June Franks, and they were to play a key part in my future. The worst part was attracting me to backing horses, which as you will hear throughout this story, has brought misery upon me. June and Jimmy loved their racing; in fact, as a girl June worked for the legendary Neville Crump at Middleham as a stable lass. She used to tell a story about Crump and it must be true because I have heard it from other sources. Neville was a captain in the Army during the war and was in Singapore and captured when it fell to the Japanese so spent the rest of the war as a POW. Years later, back in Middleham training horses, he was stopped in the street by some Japanese tourists. Middleham has an old castle which is a tourist attraction and the tourists simply wanted to ask Neville directions to the said castle. His reply was, 'You found fucking Pearl Harbour easily enough, you shouldn't have any bother finding a fucking castle.' When I joined the Army later in life I ended up in the same regiment as Jimmy, and life could not have been better until one day he dealt me a card straight off the bottom of the pack, as you will hear about later.

My father never had the same respect from me as my uncles, probably because he and my mother divorced when I was still young. We were to meet up later in life and I was at his bedside when he died. He served in the RAF during the war and was stationed in Edinburgh when he met and married my mother. As a boy he was capped for England schoolboys and looked set for a career at Newcastle United when the war broke out. Every one of his friends and my relations in Durham tell me he was a top-class left-half-back. In fact, my family and the Robson family who lived about two miles down the road were close friends, and the two families are acknowledged as producing two of the best players ever from the Durham area, Bobby Robson and my father. Sadly and unbelievably I never saw my father play and he never saw me play. He also played cricket for Durham County. Like his father, he was also a great pigeon man. In the time I spent on holidays at Ushaw Moor I was never away from the allotments, where everyone either had a garden, a pigeon loft or a greyhound kennel. I kept pigeons as a boy, but only as pets, and talked all my pals into doing the same, but I never had any interest in racing them. I would help my father and grandfather clean their lofts and tidy their allotment, but my real love and only interest was the greyhound kennels. I would pester the owners to walk their dogs and they were only too happy to accommodate me. In later life I was to own and train over 100 dogs but it all started back there.

Back in the Ferry, our boyhood days were over, we were all now working for a living, dating girls, going dog racing at Powderhall and Linlithgow and following Hearts home and away as none of us were playing football, probably because living outside Edinburgh nobody seemed to want us. When I say dating girls, apart from Lennie I can't remember any of us having a steady girlfriend. In fact, despite me telling you the close bonds everyone in the Ferry formed, only Lennie and Jimmy Liddle married local girls. We never had much luck at the Palais either, though unknown to me then I would meet my wife there later in life, and later still the pin-up girl of the Palais would become the love of my life. When we chatted to a girl at the Palais she either thought we were country hicks or wanted a boyfriend not a pen pal. Mind you, there were some stunners in the Ferry, and though we went out together it was really only teenage capers, but we had our moments. Just so they don't feel forgotten, I will mention Sheila Liddle, Mary Fox, Norah Brown, Margaret Quigley and Senga Russell (I didn't do that bad). I also remember one day the door went and there was Linda Adams and her pal asking me if I wanted to go to North Queensferry with them. Linda was a Ferry Fair Queen and everyone's pin up. The lads didn't believe me and Jock said they probably wanted someone to pay the boat fare (actually they paid). I was too shy to push my luck, but who knows what might have been. I also went out with three of the farm lads' sisters so I wasn't exactly Quasimodo.

I will finish our younger days by highlighting other events that we enjoyed and some still do. Our highlight was the Ferry Fair held on the first Saturday in August, though events lasted from the Monday to the finale on Saturday. All through the week we had the Burryman parading around the village. This was a local covered head to toe in a suit of burrs and supported by two helpers. On Friday night we had the Boundary Race, a five-mile race around the boundary of the village. I finished fourth, third and second in the times I ran in it. After the race we had the Greasy Pole in the Burgess Park. This was a grease-covered pole about 40ft high and it took some winning; I never tried it. On the Saturday morning every kid in the village would file past our house, Catherine Bank, down McIvers Brae and form a parade on the promenade. A pipe band would then lead us along the main street to the town hall for the crowning of the Fair Queen. After that we had the Burgh Race from the council chambers to the town hall. I never ran in it, but Jim O'Donnell and another lad I will mention, Davie Bonnar, both won it. The afternoon moved back to Burgess Park, where there was tug-o-war, pillow fighting and bucking bronco contests. The funfair was always provided by the Codonas. We used to pray (the football team that is) that it stayed dry, because if it didn't then we had to flatten the ruts the heavy vehicles caused. I wouldn't have minded the takings from the pubs that week, they were mobbed, but we were too young to be involved. I mentioned Davie Bonnar because he was a footballing revelation. We all went to Tynecastle to see him play for Scotland schoolboys against England and he scored a hat-trick. His entire family were Celtic mad and it was assumed he would go to Celtic, but money talked and he signed for Everton. His younger brother Andy and his cousin Raymond McMahon played in our under-16 team, and well at that, but the whole family were talented players.

To close my Ferry boyhood stories I would like to play tribute to the brilliant lads who helped create Queensferry United – united being the operative word. Richard Sandilands, Willie Easton, Micky McWilliams and Jock MacDonald, the farm lads; John Scott and Jerry McMahon our two wingers;

George Orr, Willie Shilling, Martin Scott, the Bonnar brothers and the McMahon brothers, thanks lads for all your efforts. There was one country lad who slipped our net, Colin Stein who lived in Philipstoun. All the farm lads knew him, but he went to school in Linlithgow, whereas all the others went to the Ferry school. I only mention him because later in life I was to meet Alex Ferguson, and both Alex and Colin were record signings at one time for Rangers, and in fact when Colin went to Rangers they tried to do a deal involving Alex, which he turned down. I will say this, if I had them both on hand for the under-16 side, Alex would have got the nod hands down.

CHAPTER TWO

I worked for a livestock auctioneer before joining the Army. While I was in the Stock Exchange my boss Colin Dishington invited me to play for his cricket team, Newington. This was a revelation. We were champions for the two years I was there, and every year thereafter as far as I know. It was a strange team, every one of us were good cricketers, but we seldom got a chance to show it. Colin and his pal Charlie Mann were our opening batsmen and were unbeatable, and they also did all the bowling so you could say it was a two-man team with nine fielders. Mind you, in fairness we usually had the league won half-way through the season, and when that was accomplished Colin and Charlie would step back and give the rest of us a chance. While we were boys we lived in each other's pockets, living for the day we left school and started work. Now the time had arrived we realised that life wasn't the bed of roses we were used to. Sure, we all went to Butlin's a couple of times, went camping, started venturing into Edinburgh and going to the Palais and the Locarno, but all that cost money and now we were working, but after giving our parents our keep we were always on the skint side. We did get by though as somebody always came up with a few bob.

As well as venturing into Edinburgh, we used to cross the Forth on a Sunday night to go dancing at the Burnside Club in Rosyth. The last ferry boat was at 11pm and we always caught it, except for one fateful night when we missed it. We had three options, sleep in a doorway, swim the Forth or walk 40 miles round by the Kincardine Bridge. I was a sort of ring leader and, as Del Trotter would say, I said 'Lads, the answer to our problem is staring us in the face'. 'What?' they said. 'There,' I replied, pointing to the Forth Bridge. 'Alan, they said, you must be fucking joking.' 'No,' I said, 'Kenneth More did it.' Anyway, I made my way up to the bridge approach and they followed me. Part one was easy enough, the signal box was right at the start of the bridge and easy to sneak past. Once we were on the bridge the signal man probably saw us, but he certainly wasn't going to follow us, but it was immaterial as there was a welcoming committee at the other end. Part two was the nightmare of all nightmares. It was a mild midsummer's night but the wind was like a hurricane up there. Half an hour earlier I had said why not, Kenneth More did it, referring to the film The 39 Steps when More, as Richard Hannay, gets off a train on the bridge to escape his pursuers, ending up ashore in South Queensferry. I tell you now, Kenneth More never walked on that bridge, and if he did he was dafter than us. Luckily, we made it across in one piece to find the boys in blue waiting to welcome us. The police were more worried about what the consequences could have been. We were charged with trespassing on railway property and fined £5.

A couple of weeks later one of the crowd, Willie Job, and myself were at Linlithgow dogs on a Thursday night. We emptied our pockets on a dog owned by Nel Mochan, the Celtic player, and ended up walking home. Bugger this we thought, let's get out of this, let's join the Army, which we did the next day, enlisting in the Royal Artillery.

After signing up we were eventually summoned to the training depot at Oswestry in February 1962. From here on in I am going to tell you happy stories, sad stories, funny stories and stories to please any animal lover. Basic training was OK. Willie came from a military background and fitted in straight away. I didn't find it so easy but got there. In the cross-country race for the regiment, I won and Willie was second, and we both played in the draft winning football team. The Army is a great institution, you will never beat it, and if you play the game its way it can be a great life. The first thing I learned was if you want something ask for the opposite. They asked me what position do you play, I said inside-right and they played me at right-back. On completing training they ask you your preferred posting. I asked for Craigiehall outside Queensferry and they sent me to Germany. They asked what trade I wanted. I said a PTI or some other type of instructor and they made me the last thing I wanted, a clerk, though I did get out of that.

I was posted to one of the Army's top regiments, 1st Regiment Royal Horse Artillery in Hildesheim near Hanover, and spent one year there and one year back in Scotland at JTR Troon. I loved it at Troon, it was like being back in civvy street as I was home and at Powderhall every Saturday night. I love my home city of Edinburgh, but next to Edinburgh nowhere in the world have I met anyone to come close to the Glaswegians. Later in life when I became self-employed I did well in Glasgow, but my first encounter was a stormy Sunday night when returning from a weekend at home. I missed the last train to Troon from Glasgow. It wasn't a problem, being a serving soldier all I had to do was go to the nearest police station where I could stay till the first train in the morning. There was no one around to ask directions so I hailed a taxi, and as it pulled up an elderly couple appeared from a doorway where they had been sheltering. As I was first they asked if they could share the cab. I said if they directed me to the nearest police station they could have the cab. They asked what my problem was and when I told them they said the nearest station was 200 yards away, but forget it come home with us. They made me supper, gave me a bed, got up early and gave me breakfast then ran me to the station.

To this day I have never forgotten that act of kindness and always have and will have a deep respect for Glaswegians. Throughout my life I would meet many more, and of the hundreds I know only one has been a 'wrong un'. Next to the Glaswegians would be the Geordies, Paddies, Yorkies and Lancastrians in that order. South of Manchester I didn't rate anyone much. Londoners I found arrogant, mouthy, flash and tight as ducks' arses. The Welsh I never liked, and they were even tighter than Londoners. During Army basic training we were on a forced march in Snowdonia. We passed a country house with two full milk bottles outside which we nicked and drank. Two days later we were called on parade and who was there but the house owner whose milk we had nicked. The milk was worth about 2/6d in old currency and this tight bastard drove 40 miles for his half crown.

I spent eight years in Germany and found the Germans arrogant but friendly enough considering it was only 17 years since Bomber Harris did a demolition job on them. They were clean, well presented and worked hard. The Dutch I found even tighter than the Welsh, and that is saying something. I never spent any time in Belgium, but I did in France and I detested them. The Italians? Who couldn't like them or their country. Their hotels and restaurants are so clean, and their whole attitude to life is refreshing.

I spent time in Libya and in Cyprus with the United Nations forces and I will tell you stories about these places later, but the people? I made a fortune in both Libya and Cyprus but with the Arabs, Greeks and Turks always watch your back and if you don't nail something down they will nick it.

After a year in Troon I returned to the RHA in Germany where I met another lifelong friend, Bobby Sinton. We first met each other on the ski slopes of the Hartz Mountains where we were taking part in the Regiment's skiing championship. The regiment ran a bus to the slopes every Sunday as they were only 40 miles away, and if only for nothing better to do on a Sunday we used to go mainly to eye up the talent in St Andreasburg. I actually went out with a German girl I met there but it never came to anything. We liked the skiing but never got past the novice stage. We entered for the two-man bobsleigh race. The idea was that you pushed the sledge, the anchor man – me – dived on, then the steerer – Bobby – dived on as well. In the race I missed the sledge and it shot off, Bobby jumped on top of me and down the slope we went sledgeless.

We were actually the fastest across the finish line but you had to have a sleigh to be declared winners, although we did get the dunce's award. Our next escapade came when we sent a bet to Hills back home on Noblesse to win the Oaks at Epsom and she obliged at 6-4. We had £100 on her and we got our cash and went down the town. We had been told there was a German tote betting shop in the town and we found it. I seem to have a knack for this because years later in Holland I found a Ladbrokes in both Amsterdam and Arnhem! The shop took bets mainly on French and German racing but sometimes got the British card. Anyway, this Sunday the German Derby was being run in Hamburg and Lester Piggott had a mount. We bet £100 on it and it romped in at 9-2. Between the two races we had nearly 7,000 Deutschmarks, a fortune in 1964, so instead of returning to the barracks where Sunday tea was crap anyway we decided to dine in Hildesheim's top restaurant.

We sat down and ordered in our best pidgin German, 'Zwei Hanchen und Pomfrits bitte.' Two chicken and chips please. The waiter looked at us like Manuel in Fawlty Towers. 'Vass?' he said. Bobby did an imitation of a chicken flapping its wings and laying an egg. Know what Manuel brought us? Two egg and chips.

We went to Hanover races one Sunday 40 miles the other side of Hildesheim. We got our tickets at the station, but I said just get a single, we are bound to see someone we know and get a lift back. Anyway, come the last race we were low on funds but really fancied a horse, so bold me says stick the return fare on as well (we hadn't seen anyone we knew). Bobby says 'what if it loses?' Says me, 'So what, we will thumb a lift.' The horse is ten lengths clear at the last, but falls, and we were left skint. Bobby points to the far side of the course and says that looks like Route Six, the main road to Hildesheim. Can't be, I said, we came in the main entrance, we will go out that way. We'd taken a taxi to the course from the station so really hadn't a clue where we were. We walked back towards what we thought was the station and eventually saw the signs for Route Six. We had walked five miles before arriving back at the spot Bobby had thought we should have been. We never saw a military vehicle, no German would stop for us, so we had a 40-mile walk. We ran most of it, as we were fit cross-country runners, but it was still 6am before we got back to camp.

We were both in the regimental cross-country team, but Bobby was streets ahead of me, and in fact he wasn't far short of international class. Where Bobby spent all his time training, my spare time was spent up at the regiment's stables where the officers' showjumpers were kept. National Service was still in force but coming to an end, and one of the stable lads, a National Serviceman called Tony Beaston, was a jockey with the trainer George Owen and he taught me to ride. I spent hours there whenever I could. At the stables we had a chestnut gelding called Khaled who could jump for fun when he wanted to, but when he didn't nothing would make him, not even Tony, a professional jockey. I rode him out one Saturday afternoon and what a gem he turned out to be. After that I rode him out whenever I could and what a horse he turned out to be. He ended up winning every event he was entered in. On my first leave home after returning to Germany, I was at the Palais in Fountainbridge when I met a girl called Marilyn, who I was to marry a year later and have three daughters with.

On returning to Germany I found my Uncle Jimmy McHardy had been posted there. I immediately applied to rebadge (that means join a different corps), it was approved and I was claimed, as families were allowed to do, to Jimmy's regiment. I was over the moon as I moved to my new home, 66 Squadron RASC in Nienburg, the other side of Hanover from Hildesheim. The lads there were brilliant, although I was a bit unsure at first. As I was the Quartermaster's nephew, would I be resented if I was shown any favouritism. Jimmy had me out to be some kind of superstar, which I wasn't, but I walked into the squadron football team right away. I thought this a bit unfair on the lad I was replacing as he was a good player and here he was being dropped for some unknown who had never even kicked a ball in the place. It did work out well though, I hit it off right away and the lad I replaced was back in the team in another position soon after.

Soon after arriving our Squadron took possession of a new vehicle called the Stalwart, made by Alvis in Coventry. We got 10 Stalwarts and 20 of us – 10 drivers and 10 co-drivers – travelled to Coventry, did a crash course and drove them back to Germany. It was a fantastic vehicle, six wheeled, independent suspension, amphibious and heavily armour-plated in front with bullet-proof windows. In wartime your frontline was tanks supported by infantry. Some 20 miles or so behind the frontline was the distribution point where the tank's fuel was stored. When the tanks ran low on fuel they had to stop and await trucks bringing fuel from the DP. The idea of the Stalwart, with its independent suspension, meant it could go anywhere a tank could go, so a system called 'Through Running' was devised. It meant the frontline never halted, the Stalwarts loaded with five-gallon jerry cans went everywhere the tanks went and refuelled them immediately. If, as the Germans did in Normandy, the enemy flooded ditches, the tanks would plough their way through and the Stalwarts would ferry the infantry across.

Now no one liked exercises, especially in January or February, because Germany was one cold place at that time of year. The grub was crap, all tinned stuff and you were manky most of the time. We would do manoeuvres by day and lager up at nights in farm yards or villages. With the Stalwarts it was heaven sent. There you were in a farm yard, pitch black, 2,000 gallons of petrol in your vehicle. The farm has tractors and harvesters etc, well what would you do? Tell you what I did, I flogged the petrol to the said farmers and anyone else who wanted to buy it. It was foolproof, you had 200 cans of petrol, who was going to miss 20 or 30? When you filled a tank you just poured and poured until it was full, flung the empty cans back on the Stalwart and went back for more. You went out with 200 full cans and when you came back you just slung the empties off and stocked up again. No one ever counted the empties. In fact, no one ever really counted what went on the Stalwart. It held 200 cans but depending how you stacked them it could be 190 or 210, no one ever checked.

In those days there were 12 marks to the pound and you easily made 1,000 to 2,000 marks on every exercise, so it was a nice little earner, plus the Germans couldn't get hold of British fags or tobacco so that was another earner. The only one snag I ever hit was on one occasion instead of MT74, which was the grade for tanks and trucks, I was loaded up with AVGAS, aviation fuel, and assigned to a helicopter squadron. I sold it just the same but never did hear what became of the vehicles it was used in. We did the same in Libya two years later, but that's another story.

The exercise season over and back in barracks, I had a tidy sum tucked away for my forthcoming wedding, I had proposed to my girlfriend Marilyn and all was arranged for August. To further supplement my savings my uncle got me the job of running the Sergeants' Mess bar. With tips and the extra duty pay my honeymoon was paid for. The job meant working nights, but the days were free so it gave me time to train hard for the upcoming athletics meeting with our sister squadron, 12 Squadron. As with the regimental boxing tournament, the regimental athletics meeting generates a fair amount of betting. This is where the only resentment I ever came across dug in. Once again, Jimmy had me down as winner of the 5,000 metres and to be fair he had seen me run and was confident. Problem was a lad from Edinburgh called Stan McFaul had been champion for the past two years and the other three lads in the four-man team were reported to be no slouches either. McFaul's stance was why should I walk into the team, which was fair comment. The obvious answer was to race the five of us and pick the first four, which we did. Now I had trained hard for six weeks and was spot on. When the trial began I went straight to the front and after a couple of the 12 laps I glanced back and knew right away I was a shoo-in, the rest were toiling. Bearing in mind money was going to be staked on the regimental race, I shortened my stride, let McFaul and another pass me, looked as though I was all out and finished third, securing my place. Truth was I could have won by a lap, which in fact I did when the race came along. I told Jimmy to offer 5-1 on McFaul and 10-1 on everyone else. We're not talking about fortunes, the average stake would be 20 or 30 marks, £2 or £3, but it was fun. Jimmy was a bit of a tightwad at times and wasn't sure about taking a chance, but my Aunt June loved a flutter and couldn't wait for the event. In the event, McFaul was proved right, he was better than the rest and the 12 Squadron team, but unfortunately for him he was a lap slower than me. For good measure I also won the 1,500 metres later in the day. June and Jimmy won about £50. Me? Nothing. One rule and the divine rule in the Army is you can steal anything not nailed down and it is fair game, steal from a fellow soldier and it is unforgivable. Had I taken money off my mates that day it would have been the same as stealing.

I hadn't been in my new regiment a year but life couldn't have been better. I was living beside relatives I had always thought the world of, I had plenty of new friends, I was a member of the football team who won the league and was regimental 5,000 and 1,500 metres champion. I was due to be married in 12 weeks' time and I had been allocated a married quarter before I was even married.

The only event of note before I got married happened in Hamburg. The city was devastated by horrendous floods, which resulted in many deaths. We were rushed to the floods with our amphibious Stalwarts, and although we did a lot of good I wish we could have done more. Trouble was, the Stalwarts' speed on water was only six knots and in places it was impossible to beat the current, but we did all we could and I must say our help was appreciated. It did a lot to restore relations between the German public and the Army following incidents in Minden a year or so earlier. The Cameronians, a truly great Scottish regiment, were stationed there and I know a lot more than most about the true facts as my godfather, another great soldier called Ronnie Andrews, was their RSM. What happened was Minden sits on the River Weser and was crowded with barges and the people who live on them, or bargees as they call themselves. They were a tough lot, but not as tough as the Cameronians, and there were fights every weekend which the Jocks seldom lost. One night, however, a group of bargees cornered and severely beat up two Cameronians. Big, big mistake. The boys went out in force and took the place apart. That wouldn't have been so bad as incidents like that happened most weekends in German towns, but this time, however, events back in Whitehall were to affect every soldier in Germany. The scandal involving defence minister John Profumo and call girl Christine Keeler was about to unfold and the opposition were about to reap every benefit.

As a result Minden was blown out of all proportion. The Cameronians were vilified and labelled 'poisoned dwarfs', and every serviceman in Germany had their privileges restricted. Where before you could stay out as long as you wanted as long as you were on parade the next day, now officers and senior ranks had to be back in their barracks by 2am and other ranks by midnight. Profumo resigned and the Government collapsed but the Army suffered.

Another world-shattering incident that happened during my time in Hildesheim was the assassination of President Kennedy in Dallas. A question always asked is, 'where were you when Kennedy was shot?' Bobby Sinton and I, who shared a billet, were getting ready to go on parade at 7.45am when the news came through. There are so many theories about what really happened and I have studied them a lot. There is a book by an English author, Matthew Brown, called The Second Red and I would advise anyone with an interest in the subject to read it. In fact, Sir Alex Ferguson has a copy that I sent him. Alex is not only the greatest manager ever, he is a highly intelligent man who takes time to study major events such as JFK, and after he read the book he was impressed with the findings. For what it's worth I will give you my view.

At the time my job was regimental armourer, which meant I cleaned and maintained the regiment's weapons, so there wasn't much I didn't know about a rifle, and on the ranges I was a pretty good shot. I wouldn't and couldn't have taken the shot Oswald was alleged to have taken and I don't know any marksman, sniper or infantryman who would have either.

Firstly, you were firing from a steep angle at a vehicle moving away from you. Secondly, if you had fired and hit Kennedy the bullet would have entered the back of his head and blown the front away. Jackie Kennedy is seen scrambling over the boot of the car looking at JFK's skull fragments, clearly meaning the shot came from the front, almost certainly the grassy knoll always mentioned in reports. The magic bullet alleged to have hit Kennedy and passed through Governor Connolly twice was the most absurd thing I have ever heard. Thirdly, the motorcade was to pass along the main thoroughfare and under a flyover on its way to the Conference Centre but was diverted round by the Book Depository and towards the grassy knoll. For God's sake, we are talking about the President, nothing should impede his route but it did that day. Fourthly, Oswald – we know he worked in the Book Depository but how was he fingered so quickly? Oswald was set up. He believed he was being picked up for a mission to Cuba. When he wasn't picked up at his digs he went to his alternative rendezvous, the cinema. On the way he was alleged to have shot the lone policeman and even this story isn't convincing as witness statements differ and 21 witnesses died accidentally in the aftermath of events.

So Oswald arrives at the cinema and he doesn't pay. Now this is the crazy part. Say that happened to any of us, you wouldn't be a yard past the cashier before he or she said, 'Excuse me sir, you haven't paid'. Let's say you are deaf and you don't hear her and you take your seat, she calls the manager who comes over to you and says, 'Excuse me sir, you haven't paid for your seat'. A hundred times out of a hundred you would say, 'I am so sorry I was away in a daydream,' and pay for your ticket, end of story. Let's say you were a drunk or caused an incident. The manager would have his staff eject you or at worst call the police, and who knows how long if at all it would take them to respond to such a minor incident. That day, however, there were 200 armed FBI agents and policemen swarming into the cinema within minutes of Oswald entering. Lastly, in the few words Oswald was recorded as saying, they were 'I didn't kill anyone, I am a patsy'. The next morning at the courthouse where the alleged killer of the president is being held, the security is so lax that Jack Ruby can walk in and shoot Oswald. The picture of Oswald being shot also tells a story a blind man could see. The alleged killer, the most notorious in history, is being escorted by two agents, one on either side, leaving Ruby a clear view and shot at Oswald. Look at any newspaper or TV coverage of a major criminal being escorted into or out of court and he is totally surrounded by police officers. You couldn't touch him or get anywhere near him, never mind shoot him, so doesn't the photo of Oswald's shooting speak volumes?

The English author Brown sums it up well. Kennedy was warned not to go to Dallas. The FBI and the CIA hated him as they felt he let them down in The Bay of Pigs fiasco so they had it in for him, especially as they had agents killed. He was intending to cut oil concessions which infuriated the oil barons, so Texas. never mind Dallas, wasn't the best place for JFK to be as they also had it in for him. He had instructed his brother Bobby, who was also later assassinated, to purge the Mafia, which he set about doing with a vengeance. Any one or all three of these parties could have and probably did do the deed. The Dallas District Attorney refused to release the body and demanded an autopsy, and rightly so because president or not it was a homicide in his jurisdiction. He was completely ignored, the body was sealed in its coffin and flown back to Washington immediately. One other interesting point: shortly after the shooting we were on a major six-week exercise in the American sector of Germany and naturally the subject came up in chatter in the PX, as the Yanks' canteen was called. The general opinion, and I am talking at least 80 per cent of the American soldiers, was 'good riddance to him'.

Anyway, back to the present and my wedding. It took place in Viewford Church near Dundee Street in Edinburgh where my wife Marilyn lived. Dundee Street was to be our new home when we were on leave and for three years after we left the forces. Goodbye Queensferry. I was to meet another good friend Denis Roe who also lived in Dundee Street, next door to the Connery family, Tam and Neil and their parents. Neil was the same age as Denis and me but his older brother Tam had already left home to take up his new job, in which you know him as 007, Sean Connery. In his autobiography Sean writes about our local, The Dundee Arms or Vietnam as it was often called. Dundee Street was all Scottish and Newcastle Brewery workers and on a Friday the draymen and brewery workers flocked to The Dundee Arms, and believe me it was bedlam. Kate Adie refused to enter it without body armour and an armed escort. You could buy anything in there from the Ark Royal to an acorn, but more about that later.

For all I have told you about my pals in Queensferry, only another lifelong pal Lennie Dodson and his wife Sandra were still there. I had lost touch with the farm lads and all the others moved away, though Jock and Jimmy O'Donnell would return. Bobby Sinton was my best man and another pal, a Glaswegian called Andy Meikle, also came from Germany for the occasion. Everything went well, but unknown to me it was to be the last time I was to see my youngest cousin Hilary. I was just back in Germany when I received a phone call from my mother telling me Hilly had died of a brain tumour. I was devastated, she was the cutest, sweetest little gem of an angel, who I am so sorry to say became one 70-odd years before she should have. We all know we are going to lose our parents sometime, but no parent should ever have to endure the anguish of losing a child. I know my Aunt Mary never got over it, as brave as she tried to be.

Marilyn and I settled down to married life and our first Christmas/New Year was spent in Germany only the second and last time I wasn't home. Life with the Stalwarts was hectic. Every country tied to the UN or NATO wanted them so we travelled all over showing them off. We made a film for 'Look At Life', for which the Army earned fortunes but we got peanuts in extra duty pay. We were up at all hours of the morning filming the Stalwarts appearing over the horizon and late at night filming them disappearing into the sunset. We swam in the lakes of Denmark and the fjords of Norway. Every main railway station with recruiting posters had a photo of a Stalwart manned by a local lad. In Edinburgh Waverley it was another big pal Phil Ramsay and myself on the poster. Phil and his wife Edith and Marilyn and I became close friends. Phil was our outside-left and team captain and was an absolutely brilliant player. He should have signed for Hibs but he lost his father and joined the Army to help support his mother. As I've said earlier, I'm a lifelong Hearts fan so have no time for our city rivals. In all my nine years' Army service Phil was the only Hibs fan I ever came across, plenty of Rangers and Celtic, but no Hibs – or Easter Rodents as Hearts fans refer to them.

Every time we went on exercise the Army were being hit by massive claims from German farmers for damage to their fields and crops. We honestly did as little damage as possible but you only had to touch a corner of a field and they were claiming the whole shooting match. In their wisdom, the Army decided it would be cheaper to load the tanks and infantry on LSTs and ship them to Tobruk and on into the Libyan desert to blast away to their hearts' content. An initial trial six-week exercise was mounted and our squadron was to act as the transport unit ferrying the infantry out into the desert. The next six weeks were to be Shangri La. We were under canvas at our base camp between Derna and Tobruk. We had a marquee for the Officers' Mess, one for the Sergeants' and one for the junior and other ranks. One ten-ton truck once a week was enough to supply all the messes with the wines, spirits, beer and tobacco, soap, razor blades etc needed. We formed a cartel, the Ordnance Sergeant, the Transport Sergeant, the Pay Corporal and myself. We sent two ten-tonners per day to the NAAFI supply point in Tobruk to load up with the said booze and fags and all the petrol we could nick, which was easy as the Ordnance Sergeant was in charge of the petrol dump. We sold the lot in the Arab villages on the 90km stretch between our camp and Tobruk.

Over the six-week period we amassed a fortune for 1966. The joy was we had been paid six weeks before leaving Germany in marks, and as the mess was the only place we could spend their money, all the cash went back to Germany. This was the Pay Corporal's role, he channelled as much as he could into our cartel. On our trips to Tobruk you had to have a co-driver as it would be suicidal to send a lone driver. These Arabs would slide a knife between your ribs for a packet of fags. The pay corporal came as my co-driver as you couldn't take anyone outside the cartel. All the other lads were busy ferrying the infantry back and forth to the exercise zone so no one paid any attention to me being on the permanent Tobruk run. The joy was the Arabs couldn't get enough goods, but their Libyan money was no use to us so they had to go to a bank in Tobruk to get sterling. There was an RAF base outside Tobruk at El Adem which had married quarters and also a British post office in Tobruk. The pay corporal and I would wait outside the post office and ask every serviceman or wife who went in to buy a postal order, usually £20 or £50 to avoid suspicion. We took these back to Germany where the Pay Corporal converted them back into German marks. We got a better exchange rate this way. With the petrol we sold there was no accounting, as the Ordnance Sgt took care of that, but if anyone had ever worked out the mileage on the tanks and trucks, which no one ever did, they would have found the vehicles were doing gallons to the mile. The desert can be a beautiful place or a death trap but I loved it, not only because of our profits but the experience. During the day you can boil alive and at night you can freeze to death. I remember one night looking up at a sky that was blood red. It was a beautiful sight that not even the Northern Lights could match. It's so quiet at nights you could swear you could hear the ghosts of lost soldiers from World War Two whispering. The desert is, or was then, which was only 20 years after the war ended, littered with World War Two land mines and unexploded shells. Every so often, further out in the desert, you would hear a loud bang which meant a camel or some other inhabitant had trod on a mine.

There is so much copper and brass in spent bullet cases and shell cases that if you had the time and means to amass it you could be a millionaire many times over. There is one main road in Libya which runs from Benghazi to Tobruk along the Mediterranean coast. Along this road there are hundreds of small villages where, as I said, we reaped a small fortune, but in every one the villagers were dressed the same – traditional Arab dress, but everyone had either an 8th Army or a Afrika Korps greatcoat.

The Army decided Libya wasn't such a great idea, the tanks and trucks couldn't cope with the conditions, so we loaded all the vehicles onto an LST and shipped them to a disposal depot in Cyprus then flew back to Germany richer and happier for the experience. It was also a godsend for the Ordnance Sgt because although not difficult to cover up there was one hell of a lot of petrol missing. Rather than cart the rest back to Cyprus we held a nuclear exercise and blew the lot up to create a mushroom cloud effect. Clever eh!

Before I left Germany we had been to a place called Bunde and won our Corps Cup quarter-final. The weather had been so severe while we were in Libya that no games were played, so I was back in time for the semi-final, which we won. My pals Phil and Edith had been home on leave while I was in Libya, and my wife went with them as there was no point her staying alone in Germany when she could have been at home with her parents, and in any case she was pregnant with our first child. News came through that Phil and Edith had been in a serious car accident on the way back to Germany. That was bad enough but there was to be an even worse sickener for me. We won our semi-final without Phil and he wouldn't be back for the final either. This meant the captaincy went to a guy called Blakemore, very talented but a drunk and never a 90-minute player, a fact I often voiced. The team was published the day before and I was down to play right-half. Uncle Jimmy who picked the team explained he wanted me there instead of inside-right to combat the threat of 9 Squadron's main danger man, Stuart Cruden. The morning of the game Blakemore went into Jimmy's office and said he wasn't happy with the team. As a result another pal of mine, Andy Murray (who was from Dunblane although I don't know if he was related to THE Andy), despite never having kicked a ball for the team that season, was installed and I was dropped. Had Jimmy not been a senior NCO, meaning I would have been sent to detention in the Guard Room or court martialled, I would have hammered him stupid there and then and Blakemore as well, but he was also senior to me in rank. I never forgave Jimmy and neither did his wife June or any other member of our family. It was the stupidest decision he ever made and the costliest. Andy Murray went off with cramp after ten minutes and as there were no substitutes in those days we were left with ten men. Our right-hand side was ripped apart by Cruden and his winger and we were lucky to get away with being beaten only 3-0, our first defeat in 18 months. Had Phil been fit he would have played and so would I, and though I don't say we would have won we certainly wouldn't have been disgraced. We almost got the chance of revenge the next season when we beat 9 Squadron's sister squadron, 27 Squadron, in the quarter-final, and as they had just beaten 9 Squadron 5-1 they assured us we would hammer them in the semi-final. On the day of the game we worked on the frozen pitch all morning and got it to what we thought was playable, but the referee was in two minds so he left it to the two managers to decide. We were the home side so Jimmy should have insisted the game went ahead but decided to agree with the other guy and postpone it in the interests of safety. When the game was finally played our entire team was on leave and instead of asking for a further postponement Jimmy spinelessly let the game go ahead with a reserve side that was thrashed 9-1. When the team returned from leave we picked up our winning ways and went on to win the league again.

Phil and Edith, my wife and I were sitting in my house having a drink when my doorbell went. There were a crowd of

Germans and I though the Gestapo had come for me. It turned out they were from Hanover 96 and had been watching Phil and myself and wanted to sign us. The arrangement was we would be farmed out to their feeder team Verden, 20 miles up the road from Nienburg, they would pay £250 to buy us out of the Army and take it from there. The money was almost ten times our present earnings with expenses, bonuses, schooling for our kids, it was a brilliant opportunity. It would have panned out great if not for a night of sheer stupidity by British troops. Hanover 96 were playing Manchester United in a friendly, and though we weren't playing Phil and our Verden teammates were there. Denis Law and another player who I thought was world class, Paddy Crerand, were playing – I was to meet Paddy again many years later. That night, however, the troops rioted, it was all over the British and German papers. They created havoc in the city centre and the club chairman's and other directors' Mercedes were trashed. It was Minden all over again, relations between troops and civilians hit rock bottom and Phil and I never found out if we would have made it. As bad as that night was, worse was to come a couple of months later when England and Germany met in the World Cup Final at Wembley. I had a TV which not many of us had, and I only had it because a neighbour who was being posted sold it to me cheap. Phil's family were over visiting and my wife was in Hanover Military Hospital to give birth to our first child. I visited her in the morning and then went home to watch the match with Phil and his family. Fifteen minutes before kick-off the Admin Officer came to the house and told me Marilyn had just given birth to a little girl. We watched the game, which you all know England won, and then we all went to the hospital to see the new arrival, Lorna. We came home and spent the evening celebrating the birth in my house. Just as well because it was bedlam in the town, fights in almost every pub and arrests galore. The military and civilian police had probably their busiest night ever throughout Germany. In those days we all rooted for England except when they played Scotland.

Our time in Germany was coming to an end and what a last 18 months it had been, winning the 5,000 and 1,500 metres, being dropped for the cup final, my first daughter arriving, nearly making it in senior football, nearly avenging our cup final defeat and losing my 5,000 and 1,500 metres titles due to lack of proper preparation. I didn't train as hard as I should have, mainly due to being married. My wife didn't take kindly to me going out at 6am to run six miles before I went to work and then again at night, plus I was socialising too much. In the events themselves I was second in the 5,000, albeit a full second slower than the record time I set the previous year, and I was disqualified in the 1,500 for barging and knocking over two opponents when coming in with what I thought was a winning run. The 5,000 was won by an Irish lad called Roy McMordie whose brother Eric played for Middlesbrough and Northern Ireland. He also took Phil's place in the cup final disaster so he was a bogey to me. But I drove the most modern vehicle in the world and had a family and had been to Libya. Army life had never been better and if you had told me it was to get even better I wouldn't have believed you in 1,000 years.

One last thing of note about Nienburg was that 40 miles up the road was a place called Bergen Belsen, the infamous concentration camp. I visited it and it was something. You enter the area through a row of silver birch trees but when you enter the camp itself it is barren, not a bird sings or a flower grows, a terrible foreboding place.

Most of the squadron were being posted elsewhere while new blood from the depot was coming in to replace us. The batch I was in was destined for 8 Squadron, known as the Railway Squadron, at Longmoor in Hampshire. Phil's batch went to the Maritime Squadron near Portsmouth and the rest went to Catterick. My lot, 8 Squadron, were to train for six months' active service with the UN forces in Cyprus. But before I tell you about Cyprus – what a place and what an experience it was – I can tell you how stupid my uncle was proved to be in dropping me in the cup final. The whole Corps was being rotated, which really meant the British-based went to Germany and the German-based units came home. Our new Squadron at Longmoor, football wise, was five players from 9 Squadron, six from 27 Squadron and six including myself from the other squadrons. We were spoiled for choice, but I made the team in my favourite inside-right position. It was the best team I ever played in, totally unbeatable and my new teammates who had hammered us in the cup final couldn't believe I was left out, but, hey, that's history.

Cyprus was brilliant and I had three great jobs during the tour. The first was driving the health inspector for the UN forces. We toured the whole island inspecting UN posts, and bars and restaurants which our troops would frequent. Accompanied by the Cypriot police and health authorities, we also visited all the brothels and seedy whisky girl bars. This was necessary because in the heat of Cyprus infection could be rife and the girls were issued clean bills of health or otherwise every day. The job was shortlived as my boss was posted back to the UK and the new man brought his own driver. My next job was driver to the Aide De Camp to the Force Commander, a Swedish National Service Lieutenant. His name was Savranto, a great bloke, son of a Swedish multi-millionaire and an international playboy. He had been in so many accidents he was strictly forbidden to drive so the driving was down to me. Three or four times a week flights bringing in troops from Sweden and taking the others home flew into Nicosia. Savranto was forever dating the hostesses and he rarely used the car, and never at weekends. When we were off duty at weekends we were free to do as we pleased and the majority of the lads headed for the beaches at Famagusta, Aya Napa or Kyrenia. There's not a lot of spare staff cars available as we were an active service unit and taxis, though reasonable enough, were still not cheap. But, as I said, Savranto never used our car at the weekends so in effect I had my own car. I had no interest whatsoever in lying on a beach all day, so I used to hire the care out to the senior NCOs, a nice little earner that paid my day's racing. Sadly, with two months of my tour still left, Savranto finished his National Service and went back home, and again his replacement brought his own driver.

My last job was for a horsey man like me and it was like having Christmas every day. I was to drive a retired Brigadier who lived in Kyrenia and couldn't drive any more to and from the races every Sunday and to and from the stables complex when he wished. It turned out he was only the handicapper and senior steward of Nicosia Racing Club. He stood no nonsense and if a trainer didn't run his horse to within what the Brigadier thought was a fair relation to his assessment he would suspend him for a fortnight. The horses ran pretty straight and in two months I never had a losing Sunday. At the track, unlike the UK, the tote takes a 10 per cent cut before the race, so a £100 to win bet costs you £110. One Sunday I had £100 on a long odds on shot and got £105 back, you could have heard my cursing and swearing back home but it didn't do any good. The Brigadier and I both knew our horses and we had some great exchanges. Lester Piggott was on Sir Ivor 3-1 for the 2,000 Guineas and 6-1 for the Derby. We both thought the colt a certainty for the 2,000, but the Brigadier didn't think he would stay the Derby distance. I eventually talked him round, saying maybe on paper he won't get the distance but he will with Lester on board. At that time in the News of the World William Hill advertised their ante-post prices, 3-1 for the 2,000 and 6-1 for the Derby, special odds the double. At multiple odds we would expect 27-1 but special we thought would be a bit more. We staked a £100 win each on both races and a £50 double each. We got our 3-1 and 6-1 singles but we both hit the roof when we saw our special odds as a miserly 5-2. How crazy and crooked was that? The horse was 3-1 for the 2,000 and hadn't even won. In the event he did, and was cut to 3-1 for the Derby. Each of our £50 doubles had a £50 single on the 2,000 and we collected £200 and placed that on the revised odds for the Derby, for which we would collect £800, but William Hill wanted to pay £175. The Brigadier was livid. It cost a fortune in those days to phone the UK but he used the racing club office phone and called William Hill's head office, the Jockey Club, the BPA and eventually got satisfaction. Our single bets stood anyway, but regarding the double they reluctantly agreed to pay our double as a single at 3-1 with the option to bet the horse in another single for the Derby at the revised odds. We took our winnings on the single and did put it on the Derby, but not with William Hill. The Brigadier went elsewhere and even got us 7-2. That job took me to the end of our tour and I was sorry to say goodbye to the Brigadier as he was to see my go. He did, however, say if I ever returned to Cyprus to come and stay with him. I did return years later and did look him up but sadly he had passed away. I was, however, warmly welcomed at the racing club.

There were four other incidents during our tour that will stick in my mind forever. Firstly a quick history. Cyprus, beautiful island as it is, has been ravaged by civil disputes between Greek and Turkish Cypriots. Britain ruled and policed the island until February 1959 when we had enough of bombings, riots, murders and anything else you care to name. But we retained our sovereign bases in Dekhelia and Akrotiri. In the 50s and 60s Archbishop Makarios and his puppet general George Grivas instigated the troubles with their Enosis demands. Enosis means union with Greece, and Grivas's murderous EOKA terrorists. On 16 August 1960, Cyprus became a republic; Makarios was elected president. Sir Hugh Foot, the departing British Governor, made a plea for peace to reign but it would never be. In 1964 21 were killed in clashes between Greeks and Turks, 1,500 British troops and a UN force were flown in. The British troops were involved in heavy fighting before returning to Britain and handing the melting pot over to the UN. Clashes, murders, riots still continued, and ex-Governor Foot, the Queen, and the American President LB Johnson all appealed for peace to no avail.

Just after my lot arrived in January 1968, Grivas took his artillery into the hills between Nicosia and Kyrenia and opened fire on an innocent Turkish village to provoke an incident. The papers back home said a donkey and a few chickens were killed, but in fact four civilians were killed and Grivas made a big mistake. One of his shells hit a nearby UN post; luckily there were no casualties, and that was the UN's chance to arrest the murderous bastard. A UN team including some of our squadron were sent to arrest the thug, which they did. He and his thugs were brought back to the UN HQ in Nicosia and held under arrest until they were deported back to Greece. The second incident happened, would you believe, in a football match in the National Stadium in Nicosia. Spurs had some Cypriot connection to the board of directors and they decided to give the players an end-of-season break and play two exhibition games against the Greek Select and the Turkish Select to try and help the peace process.

We tried to get a game for the UN Select but it didn't happen. They stayed at the Famagusta Beach hotel in Famagusta and, though it was highly unlikely they would be in any danger, the UN kept a close protective eye on them. That gave me my chance to meet my boyhood hero Dave Mackay, and we exchanged a few brief words, like I am from Edinburgh and a Hearts fan and my parents live 800 yards from your parents. I never dreamed that years later we would become very close friends. If Spurs had played the UN Select I would have been playing directly against Davy and what an experience that would have been, but at least I was to enjoy the next best thing.

Anyway, Spurs enjoyed their holiday, played their games and went home to prepare for the new season. Back in Cyprus, it was felt the two games did contribute something to the peace process, so it was decided the UN Select would play the same two teams as a further goodwill gesture. Our entire squadron team were in the squad, that's how good we were, and it was made up by two Swedes and three Danes, national servicemen who were professionals and full internationals back home. After much arguing, and as I was team captain and most vociferous, it was decided we would start with the entire 8 Squadron team. I felt that they were good as they were; the Danes and the Swedes wouldn't make any significant difference. They weren't pleased but they did come on as substitutes at some point in the games, so everyone played. In the first game we beat the Greek Select 7-0 in a one-sided game that went off without incident. The second game was played in the same national stadium in Nicosia. It was an ill-tempered affair from the start and two thirds of the way through, with us leading 5-0, our inside left Lennie Finn clashed with a Turkish player near the touchline. A fan burst from the crowd, spat on Lennie and called him a 'black bastard'. Lennie decked the guy and was then attacked by more fans. I was only a few yards away and Lennie's brother Trevor was just behind me. I piled in to help Lennie and then one of the Turks pulled a knife. Trevor felled the guy with a vicious punch (he was BAOR heavyweight champion). Bedlam then broke loose. The Turkish players started fighting on the pitch with our players – big mistake – we could take it but boy could we dish it out as the Turks found to their cost. To make matters even worse, the Turkish fans started fighting among themselves and then the UN fans in the crowd joined in. It was 45 minutes of chaos until the UN Military Police arrived, followed by the Cypriot Police. Order was eventually restored and the match was abandoned.

The aftermath was in their reports to the UN. MPs and the Cypriot Police (all Greek) all damned the Turkish fans as 'savages', the Turks claimed victimisation and it was another chapter in the never-ending dispute.

Midway through our tour, Hearts reached the Scottish Cup Final. I was still driving Lt Savranto at the time so I decided to fly home. Now the rule was, unless the circumstances were compassionate, no one would be allowed home leave. Since I didn't work weekends and was detached from the squadron in my duties with Lt Savranto, I figured it didn't apply to me. I even cleared with Lt Savranto in case by any chance he needed me. I was at Nicosia airport waiting to buy my ticket when who appeared but my CSM and a couple of his sergeants, who I had promised my car for the weekend, and they were in fact in my car. The CSM was a great bloke, one of the best sergeant majors I ever served under. 'Jock,' he said, 'I know what you are doing but please don't. I won't stop you but think of the consequences.' Lt Savranto had inadvertently let it slip out, not knowing I wasn't supposed to go. 'Just jump in the car, son, and I will give you a lift back to camp before we go to Famagusta.'

The situation was averted and the mood lighthearted. I said, 'Thanks sir,' and added, considering it was my car, 'Will I drive or will you manage?' The matter was never mentioned again and it was just as well I didn't go as Hearts lost 3-1.

Next was a pleasant experience and an honour. A Canadian major approached me and asked if myself and any of our team would come and coach his team. The NPSL in America was taking off and Canada was trying to follow suit. We started work at 6am and finished at 12noon. The afternoons were too hot to train, so in the evenings I took Trevor and Lennie Finn with me – Lennie and me to coach the forwards and half-backs and Trevor the defenders. They were mustard keen and learned quickly. They improved so much that we gave them a game with our squadron team. It would have been too one-sided so we split the teams in half – it was great fun and a real boost to the Canadians' confidence. In gratitude, the Canadians couldn't do enough for us – they wined and dined us like lords, offered us extra duty pay which we refused and gave us maple leaf mementoes. They offered us a tour of the island and the Mediterranean in one of their air squadron's helicopters. Two things I don't like are helicopters and motorcycles so I declined, but Trevor and Lennie jumped at the chance. They were trained parachutists so they also got a shot at freefall parachuting. I did take up one offer though, and what an experience. One of the lads we coached was a fighter pilot and he got permission to take me up in his jet. We flew to the top of the Med, along the Turkish coast, down the Syrian, Lebanon and Israel coasts, past the Egyptian, Libyan and Tunisian coast, past Algiers, through the Straits of Gibraltar and out over the Atlantic. We turned and came back through the Straits, past the Spanish and Italian coasts and Malta, past the Greek coast, where we turned for home passing over Crete. What an experience and what would that cost?

So that was Cyprus. I never forgot it and always kept a lookout for news on the political situation. Sadly, it never changed and in July 1974 full scale war broke out. Turkish armour landed at Kyrenia and pushed inland. All tourists were evacuated into the service bases at Akrotiri and Dekhelia, among them David Nixon and the Celtic captain David Hay. Fighting was fierce but eventually Turkey got some gains and another treaty was signed. Makarias died in 1977 – good riddance – but before that Turkish leader Rauf Dinkash declared Turkish Cyprus independent. Another Turkish invasion was launched, this time landing at both Kyrenia and Famagusta. Kyrenia was destroyed and the Greeks fled Famagusta. Turkey claimed the territory and that was the last conflict. The Greeks built Aya Napa, now a thriving tourist town, and Kyrenia was rebuilt and opened again to tourism. I went back with Elaine years later and it seemed peaceful enough, so, although you never know, it does seem that the violence of the past is over.

Back at Longmoor, with just over a year left to serve in the Army, I wangled a posting back to Craigiehall near Queensferry on the grounds my mother-in-law was ill, my wife had to stay at home to look after her and needed my help. She was ill but wasn't staying with us, she was living elsewhere, and I wouldn't stay under the same roof as her. I wouldn't say she was an old cow, but when she auditioned for a part in a farmyard scene she was rejected on the grounds that when they milked her she produced pasteurised alcohol. Satan's sister, I called her.

When I arrived at Craigiehall I got a married quarter right away and no one ever asked what happened to my compassionate grounds. My second daughter Eileen was born while I was at Craigiehall and my third, Diane, a year later, but by then the cracks in my marriage were widening by the day. Halfway through my time at Craigiehall, the General Officer Commanding Scotland, Gen Norman Lusk's driver, had to undergo a back operation and I was asked to drive the general for my last few months. One of my first jobs was to pick up some bigwigs from the Cabinet Office in London and take them out to Craigiehall. Their overnight sleeper from London arrived at 6am and the first of the party I met was a great man I had come across in Germany in a cross-country race between the Argylls and the 1st RHA. His name was Colin Mitchell, Mad Mitch of Aden fame, ex-CO of the Argylls. He was now a civilian, but when I saw the looks on the faces of his party and picked up parts of their urgent conversation in the car, I knew something big was afoot. I was soon to find out.

The Ugandan dictator Idi Amin had almost bankrupted his country and was threatening to print his own currency. Despite all our and other governments' pleas about the insanity of his plan, he was adamant he would only talk to General Lusk, for whom he had been batsman during his time in the Army. Colin Mitchell and his party had come to discuss how and when the general would tackle the problem. Obviously, as his driver, myself and his aide went where the general went. As a serving soldier I signed the Official Secrets Act and am still bound by it so I can't say a lot except that the general sorted things out, but it was a scary time for him.

Although still in the Army, it was around this time I got my first greyhound. Aberdeen track was closing down and selling their dogs so my first greyhound was a black dog called Caravan Hill. My boss General Lusk had come up through the ranks and was a real soldiers' man who still preferred a night with the lads rather than in the Officers' Mess, and he came with me a couple of times to Thornton and Kirkcaldy as he also liked a flutter.

When I arrived at Craigiehall, the football team was no better than average, certainly not good enough to win anything. The RSM had never won anything in all his years running teams and told me to do my best to win something before he left the Army the next year. Because Craigiehall had hundreds of civilians as well as military personnel, there was a rule somewhere, or did I make it up, that civilians could represent the command team. I immediately recruited all my pals from Queensferry and formed a good team. The military lads weren't pleased as they lost their places, but they did get a game in the minor league midweek games. They could not have played weekends anyway as they used to go home. We said the local boys were related to the civilian workers and got away with it. We won a local minor cup, which pleased the RSM immensely, but we never really stood a chance of winning the Northern Command Army Cup, though we did reach the semi-final. It was at Craigiehall that I received the only bad injury of my career. It was playing Lothian and Borders Police and a clash on the halfway line between their centre-half and myself resulted in us both sustaining cracked ribs and concussion. Even then I only missed two games as snow and frost caused numerous postponements while I was recovering.

There was one game at Craigiehall when I was to get the biggest humiliation of my footballing life. I got a call from the Navy asking us for a game. As it was a Wednesday afternoon game I had to play all the Army lads. We played at their park Lochinvar, which was beside Jock's farm. In the Army, if they can, they keep their best players at home and that forms the Army team. You then have the Army BAOR, Army Middle East and Army Far East. The Navy keep their players on one ship and in this case it was the Ark Royal based in Rosyth. So here we are a rag tag minor units Army team playing the entire Navy team so as you can imagine we got slaughtered.

I even suggested at half time we split the teams to make it more competitive but they wouldn't have it. They had been at sea for four months and needed match practice but what they could have gained from that one-sided affair I don't know. We did get another game with the Navy when I had all the civvies available, but as the Ark had left Rosyth it wasn't the same side, although at least we won.

Craigiehall also let me catch up with my cousins, Ian, Ally and Mike Pauley and John Bell. Ian was more of a rugby player, playing for Linlithgow, but on the football park he forgot the rules were different and I had the bruises to show it. There were also two female cousins, Moira and Nan, who will kill me if I don't mention them. A local lad and another great friend Jimmy Liddle formed a mini league involving the pubs and factories in Queensferry. All the old Queensferry United boys were involved, although with different teams, as were my cousins. It was fun and brought a footballing interest back to the town it had now grown into.

There are one or two other things worth mentioning from my time at Craigiehall. There were more civilian drivers, all ex-soldiers, and an ex-MT Sgt ran the show. He made sure the civvy drivers got the best jobs but that changed when I arrived as MT Corporal and we clashed immediately. When I gave the serving soldiers the best jobs he stormed into my office saying I am an ex-MT Sergeant, I run this place. I said that's right, EX MT Sergeant and a civilian and you WERE in charge until the position could be filled by a serving soldier as it now has by me. I told him to fuck off and keep out of my way, so he went to the CO Captain Brown who more or less told him the same thing, it was a military unit not a civilian benevolent fund. The incident did have its repercussions for me though. As I told you in Germany and Libya I wasn't averse to making a bob or two on the side flogging petrol when it came to hand. Here came the opportunity of a lifetime. I was MT Corporal and in charge of all things MT, including the petrol pumps. Jerry cans were only used on exercises. Every vehicle in the Army had a work ticket which relates to its journey, time in, time out, mileage at start and end and the amount of fuel used. Now say a truck filled up to 20 and $1/10^{th}$ gallons, if you put it down at 20 you were going to show a deficit, so you entered to the roundest figure upwards, so 21 gallons went on the work ticket. We had two 1,000 gallon tanks, which I checked every morning with a massive dipstick. All these ½ and ¾ gallons would mount up leaving you a surplus. The paperwork would show a 1,000 gallon empty tank, so I simply transferred the surplus petrol into jerry cans and stored them in a flameproof stone building I used to store our engine oil, and, as my customers queued up for half-price petrol, sold it accordingly. It was simplicity itself and infallible, or so I thought. The tanker simply turned up and filled the tank and that was that. The surplus had been siphoned off and stored away so we started the process again with the new tank.

It came to an end when the civvies got their own back. Back in Germany, when my wife was in hospital having Lorna, one of my neighbours, Pete Girvan from Dunblane, would run me up to BMH Hanover to see my wife and daughter so I owed the family a favour. My doorbell went one night and there was Pete's brother James who was being posted into Craigiehall to replace me. He was on his way home to Dunblane, skint and low on petrol, without enough to get home. He had taken over his married quarters but was still on leave which was how he knew I was at Craigiehall. I told him to come around at 5am the next morning and I would fill his car up, which he did. However, I forgot I had given one of the civvy drivers a shitty 6am job and need I tell you he spotted us and shopped me. Imagine an untraceable fiddle being exposed by a simple mistake. When summoned by Captain Brown I told him the truth, which he respected me for, and as I only had a couple of weeks left to do we papered it over with a fine. It wasn't a good start for James though, he hadn't even reported for duty and was in deep trouble. Here is an example of how soldiers stick together and mind each other's back. Brilliant officer that Captain Brown was, and bearing in mind I didn't try to bullshit him but told the truth we worked a wee bit of a strategy. The civvy driver had only reported seeing me filling up the car, James was there but I was adamant (as agreed with Captain Brown) that it was me and me alone who was present, so I was charged and James got a clean start in his new posting. Captain Brown had come through the ranks himself and knew the score, how the scam worked, but he took no action, he just put one of the civvies on the petrol pump. Over the years he probably did something similar himself. You may think it crooked, and it was, but these are the perks of the job and there isn't a soldier in history that ever looked a gift horse in the mouth when it comes to a bit of fiddling. Believe it or not it's as big an offence to be overstocked as it is to be understocked so my 1,000 gallons was mine to hide. In fact, going as far back as World War Two there was an occasion in Italy when an entire train loaded with supplies went missing. There must have been millions of cartons of Lucky Strikes and other American luxuries that found their way onto the streets and into the pubs, clubs, restaurants and whatever in London, Rome, Paris and any Allied city for that matter. Soldiers' perks.

Craigiehall saw the end of my nine-year stint as a soldier, and although I was never going to do the full 22 years I still would not have missed the experiences I had for a king's ransom. It's many years since I left the Army and things are obviously different nowadays, but I would never dissuade any youngster from joining, just try for the best position/regiment available. The Army looks after its own and always has. Some facts and stories all true. Every year every unit has its annual admin inspection. This is where the term Bull comes in. Everything that doesn't move is painted or polished, anything worn or damaged is scrapped. Every unit gleams like a new pin. At the end of it all, a general comes along, inspects the parade, looks at a bit of paperwork and that's it for another year. It does, however, cover up all the various fiddles here and there. Me and my 1,000 gallon tank of petrol, for example. I don't want you thinking we were some kind of military Mafia, it was just the perks of the job.

My days in the sun were the Stalwarts in Germany and the jerry cans in Libya because although the Arabs used the petrol they wanted the cans for carrying water. How they got the smell of petrol out of them God only knows. We did have jerry cans for water but they were taboo, you could not get hold of them. Cigarettes, tobacco and booze were their other priorities and there was nothing in regulations to say you couldn't give or sell an Arab a carton of fags or a bottle of Johnnie Walker – mind you, I don't think a ten-ton truck load was envisaged. Everyone had their corner. In Germany the engineers would use their plant equipment when on exercise to do 'homers' for the farmers. At Longmoor the railway soldiers flogged copper and steel. In Cyprus the UN engineers flogged cement to the Turks. In Germany just about every soldier sold fags to the bars, clubs and brothels as the German brands were like camel dung. I seldom went down to the town so I never had any dealings in that respect, and I came home on leave every three months so I just saved up for that, but no one every bothered about making a few bob from the Germans. You had the odd money lender, which I never believed in, and now and again you would get someone making a book. Behind everything you had the main people, the Adjutant, the RSM and the Quartermaster. The Adjutant decided the day-to-day running of the Regiment and the RSM enforced it, and the QM fed and clothed us, and well at that, as an army marches and fights on its stomach. Outside of the Regiment, you had the Military Police, although contrary to belief they were not there to make life difficult. Top of the tree, of course, was the Commanding Officer, who was ultimately judged on his regiment's performance and signed off all decisions but seldom acted without consulting his Adjutant or RSM first, and that's how the Army functioned. In all my years of service I never saw a bad Adjutant, RSM or Quartermaster.

Despite cuts and confusion from various pacifists, they do a great job considering they have not lost a conflict since the end of World War Two. I remember in the 60s the anti-military brigade were having a field day after Minden, the Profumo scandal and anything else they could dig up. The Press, to their eternal credit, went for the jugular in defence of the Army. One national paper carried a front-page headline from the Kipling poem: 'It's Tommy this and Tommy that and chuck him out the brute, but it's saviour of his country when the guns begin to shoot'. Occasionally you got a daft decision, and one I remember was when somewhere down the line NCOs had to have their Army Certificates of Education to retain their rank. This was crazy – some soldiers might not have been the brightest light academically but were first-rate soldiers. Imagine an infantry sergeant with his platoon pinned down by the Taliban in Afghanistan. I would reckon a mortar or rocket launcher would be somewhat more useful than a Certificate of Education.

When I went on my three-week educational course it was a doddle. We had six MP Cpls and Sergeants on the course and what a great lot they were. If anyone was finding the course difficult we would all get together at night and help the slower ones. Everyone passed the course with high marks. When I returned to my own unit my pal Phil and another pal Johnny Warner were due to go on the same course to retain their rank.

I spent hours helping them prepare and got my thanks when they finally passed and secondly when the Education Officer phoned me to say I had done a great job preparing them. Mind you, the way the lads on my course applied themselves impressed the said Education Officer. I asked him what subjects I should help Phil and Johnny with in relation to their exams. Without actually telling me the questions they would be getting in their exam, he more or less told me enough to make sure they passed, which they did. That's the Army, mates stick together and help each other. When later in life I was to run my own business and enjoy enormous custom from the Army, I always asked to see the RSM first and seek his permission to trade with his Regiment. I was never refused and when you have the blessing of the RSM you are made.

Back to how soldiers and their families increased their income though, some regiments actually owned their own farms and with the profits were able to provide their men with better sporting kits etc than the normal issue. Some blokes would buy equipment and do picture framing, some would take up photography, the lazier lads would pay mates to do their kit.

When I was at Craigiehall and bought my first greyhound, the Scots Greys who were also stationed in Edinburgh did the same. They bought a dog, renamed it The Scots Grey and ran it in Powderhall, giving the lads and families a lot of fun. For my part, in Germany before I got married I would babysit regularly and do kits. If you weren't going down the town and blowing your wages these extras paid my expenses when I went on leave. One real earner I had – and this made me doubly popular when I joined my uncle's regiment – was a special dye I came across. When I met the German girl I mentioned in St Andreasburg I became very friendly with her brother, who was doing his national service but on civvy street was a professional footballer with Hamburg. When they 'bulled' their boots instead of using the British method of spit and polish, which took hours, the Germans used 'Strabhelene'. You simply dipped a brush in the bottle and painted it on the boots and the results were amazing. When I arrived at Nienburg, before our first big parade, it took me minutes to do my boots. To my new mates it must have been like the Indians seeing the first Iron Horse cross the Plains. There was a steady stream into my room: 'Jock, any chance?' Always the super salesman, I said, 'Come on lads, this stuff isn't cheap and if I was to do all your boots it would defeat the purpose, I would still be taking the same time as spit and polish.' Appetites whetted, of course we will pay you was the call. A big bottle of Strabhelene cost me 15 marks, lasted me months and I got 10 marks (less than £1) for each pair of boots. That was a lovely wee earner for my entire stay in Nienburg. Every single member of the Regiment from the CO down used me. I used to take the label off the bottle so no one knew what it was, but if they had really delved deep enough they could have bought it themselves. Hey, never look a gift horse in the mouth.

Another Army perk which may interest any readers, although I don't know if it still exists, is the Ordnance Depot at Stirling. Back in my day, all Army surplus stock was auctioned off there once a month. Some of the bargains were unbelievable. You could get anything from an ambulance to a pair of tweezers. I was only there a couple of times on duty but it amazed me what you could buy.

As you will read later, I was to train my greyhounds with Bill Dalrymple at Dreghorn Barracks and it was here that we were to discover our own copper mine. Close to our kennels was the live firing range; in fact, we walked our dogs over them every night. The ranges were not in constant use but when they were didn't we clean up. Every spent cartridge case is gathered up and accounted for at the end of firing, but what about the bullet head? That passes through the target and embeds itself in the sand beyond. After a day's firing, Bull and I would get the Land Rover and a couple of shovels, dig out the spent bullets and – bingo – scrapyard next stop. One particular day we got £400 worth of copper and lead, went to Wallyford with our three runners and thought a dozen Christmases had come at once.

The Officers and Sergeants Messes were forever having some function or other and the buffet they laid on was something else. Whole salmon, skinned and ready to spoon, trays of pork, sirloin, sometimes lobster, and God knows how many salads and trimmings, strawberries, cream, you name it they had it. One night I was duty Sgt and on my rounds I noticed the door to the Officers' Mess kitchen was open. The cook was away on his break and hadn't shut the door. The temptation was too much. Two black bin bags with one whole salmon and two trays of sirloin were on their way elsewhere. There was so much grub laid out it probably wasn't missed, but if it was the cook couldn't say anything without dropping himself in it. There were a lot of foxes round the camp so if it was missed it might have been put down to that. It was a fox alright, but a two-legged one.

There were a couple of much more serious stories. The first was back in Nienburg in the married quarters. A young couple were given the quarter next door to me and were trouble from day one, screaming and shouting at all hours. I felt sorry for the young wife and kid as they were forever sporting bruises, and the wife was a really nice girl who didn't deserve the bullying bastard she was lumbered with. It was so bad one night that our upstairs neighbour and myself thought he was killing them. We had to kick the door in and what a state the poor girl and kid were in. We gave the bastard a real going over, arrested him and called the Medical Officer. Anyway, the girl was sent home ASAP for her and her child's safety and the arsehole was given 28 days in the guard house. He had complained about the beating we gave him but it was put down to resisting arrest. The Army being the Army decided to send boyo on an anger-management course on his release, only he went out one night while on the course and murdered a local prostitute. Now the Army always looks after its own but not this bastard. He was to be tried under German law, but a problem arose in that anyone under 21 is considered a minor and this shit was six months short. What did the Army do? Messed him around from pillar to post for six months then handed him back to the Germans to get the maximum sentence.

The other unfortunate incident came at Longmoor. At the time the Press was rife with stories of espionage and a couple of arrests had been made so everyone was on guard. One Monday the Chief Clerk failed to return from weekend leave so alarm bells started ringing. Longmoor was well named, miles and miles of moor and forest, and when no trace was found of the Chief Clerk a search party was formed to search the moors. When I left on Thursday to go home for the weekend there was still no trace, but when I returned on the Monday I learned he had been found hanged. That didn't half spark a panic. Document after classified document that the Chief Clerk had access to was taken out onto the moor and burned to ash, but when the dust settled it didn't appear any damage had been done. It's hard to figure out how someone could betray their country, and not only their country but their family and friends as well. No riches or rewards could ever tempt me down that road, but it has happened throughout history and thankfully it is still a hanging offence.

There were another couple of stories from Craigiehall concerning the greatest soldier I ever knew – my boss General Norman Lusk. It was a Friday afternoon, about 5pm, when we got a call asking for a police escort to Berwick. What had happened was a Corporal serving in the Far East had got the heartbreaking news that his wife had suffered a brain tumour and was critically ill in Berwick Hospital. The General and I had been up since 5am as we had picked up his daughter and his girlfriend from the airport on return from holiday. The General's Bentley was the fastest car in the command and he put it at my disposal. He said you have had a long day Jock, I will get another driver, but I said no way I will do it. I picked up the Corporal at Turnhouse and with a police escort and lights flashing we made it to the hospital in 40 minutes. Fortunately his wife was still hanging on, and I am glad to say she did pull through, but neither the General or myself will ever forget the thanks we got from the family. I used to study all the World War Two battles and would ask the General for his opinion as he was involved in many of them. Funnily enough, I never rated Montgomery and neither did Norman. He thought he was bold when caution was the better option and cautious when aggression was the order of the day. Alamein was his finest hour, but a lot of the work had already been done and the Americans' entrance was the clincher. In Normandy he thought Montgomery took too long to take Caen. Arnhem should have seen him removed from Command and he let Patton beat him across the Rhine. Arnhem was a total disaster. Years later Elaine and I drove up the Nimigen to Arnhem road in a Fiat bubble car and had to pull over to let a bike pass, so how Montgomery expected to take 20,000 armoured vehicles up it was beyond comprehension. General Lusk and another great soldier Jim Davidson, the RSM of the Scots Guards, were both of the same opinion. After Normandy a broad front should have been used and was reverted to anyway after the debacle at Arnhem. The idea of Arnhem was to lay a carpet of Allied paratroopers, two American Divisions, British airborne and the Polish airborne, for 30 Armoured Corps to move over, cross the Rhine and sweep into the industrial heart of Germany, ending the war by Christmas. It was a disaster and Montgomery virtually sacrificed the British airborne. According to my General, Montgomery was lucky that Hitler had a bad habit of countermanding his generals and defending the indefensible. Holland was lost and what Norman Lusk would have done was let 30 Corps cross the Rhine at Arnhem then blow the bridge (which they did later anyway). That way the Germans would have an entire armoured corps trapped on the wrong side of the Rhine and open to annihilation. If that had happened it would have been the ultimate humiliation of Montgomery. As I said, General Lusk was a soldier's soldier and he was as at home in the NAAFI playing darts and snooker with the lads as he was in the Officers' Mess. One dislike he had, like every soldier, was his deep hatred for the pacifist Labour MP Tam Dalyell. Norman never forgave him for his anti-army views. By the time the Falklands War came along I was long out of the Army, but Dalyell really went over the top in that campaign.

To end my serving days a last couple of stories and facts. Every so often some smart arse comes up with the subject of bullying and racism in the Army. Bullies were always dealt with savagely and I never saw any racism. In the RHA there was one coloured lad, 20-odd Fijians at Nienburg, none at Troon, two at Longmoore and none at Craigiehall. Not a lot, but every one was a decent, hard-working and good soldier. True, in basic training, which is only three months, you are bounced from pillar to post, but that's the Army's way of installing the meaning of discipline into a soldier. When you join your regiment it's a different ball game. If you can't take basic training, you can buy yourself out for £20, and £250 after training, at least that's the way it was in my day. Two main armies (I will exclude the Russians) won the war. America came in late, didn't have the British discipline and were racist. They would not allow a coloured soldier to serve in a front-line infantry regiment until October 1944, when a squadron of coloured tankers joined Patton. There were no front line coloured men in ETO, they were used as supply drivers, cooks, dogsbodies etc, so there you had it. The most powerful democratic nation on the planet fighting the worst racist in history with a segregated army. Be that as it may, when they joined the greatest army in the world (the Tommies) victory was assured. One last story about the Americans, when I was at Troon they were based at Prestwick and we arranged inter-unit mess games nigh. One night a Yank asked me, 'Why ain't you limeys in Vietnam?' I replied, 'As far as I'm aware the Vietcong haven't asked us for any help yet'. You don't want to know what followed but there were no more games nights.

CHAPTER THREE

Now back in civvy street, our local was the Barnton Hotel, and there I met the Bissett brothers, Eddie and Willie, who were greyhound men. They brought me two of their dogs, Funcheon Missile and Hunday Bay, both potential open racers. Funcheon was to become my best-loved dog and Hunday Bay was probably the fastest dog potentially ever, but boy was he kinky. Later I would have two blistering-paced dogs that were placed in the English and Irish Derbies respectively. They would beat Hunday Bay in a race but I doubt if they would have matched his early pace. We sorted him out eventually but by then he had turned four and his best days were behind him. In his early days he would lead by lengths then wait for the other dogs, play around, pass them again, stop again and so on. He would win, but handicappers just didn't want him on their card. He calmed down as he got older but his chance had gone.

By now I was living on Dundee Street and I went into partnership with an older bloke called Bobby Christie, whose lease on his kennels had expired. We built kennels in my backyard and moved the dogs in. Bobby had eight and I had my two. We were soon forced to move again as the brewery got a compulsory purchase order on our block. We got a new site quickly enough, but while our new kennels were being built we had to find temporary homes for our dogs. Funcheon

Missile, or Joey as his pet name was, went to a couple at Newbridge a couple of miles outside Edinburgh, and here is a story for the animal lovers. Joey was my favourite but I was also his. I was devastated when I got a call telling me he had escaped from his kennel at Newbridge. I drove out and looked everywhere but there was no sign of him. Despondent, I drove home but got a glimmer of hope that night when I got a phone call to say a dog resembling Joey had been hanging about the Armadale track but no one could catch him. I drove out right away, but again there was no sign of him. I returned home and feared he was lost when I heard nothing for two days. By this time I was driving a mobile bakery van for a local bakery and I came home from work to find a cold, tired, hungry but happy Joey waiting on my doorstep. He had gone 20 miles to Armadale, where he raced, looking for me and then found his way back 30 miles into Edinburgh. What a dog.

We still went to Powderhall every Thursday and Saturday but raced our dogs on the flapping circuit. I became friendly with a real greyhound man, Bill Dalrymple, with whom I was later to form the best and most successful partnership you could imagine. Bobby and I moved into our new kennels and bought some new dogs from Ireland and for a year or so everything ran smoothly until Bobby announced a friend of his wanted us to train one of his dogs. I didn't particularly like the bloke but, as he was a friend of Bobby's, as long as he paid his fees it wasn't a big deal. However, he started turning up at the kennels more often and making out he was part of the partnership. The split came one night at Wallyford.

I had Joey spot on and expected him to win, which he did, and we also expected this other guy's dog to oblige. When I asked him did he want to pool his cash with us or do his own thing, he replied, 'The dog's not trying.' When I asked what he was havering about, he said he had been down to the kennels earlier and stopped the dog. I asked how he had managed that and he said, 'Bobby gave me a key.' I told him to take his dog away and if I ever saw him near the kennels again I would put my boot so far up his arse he would be tasting leather for the foreseeable future. The outcome was Bobby didn't like his pal being threatened and I didn't like their conduct so we split. I took Joey and my other dogs and left Bobby with Hunday Bay and his dogs. He was well off but a tight old bastard who thought he was getting off lightly. I told him first thing tomorrow I want £500 for my share of the kennel or it gets torn down and burned.

He came across with the cash but still got the best of the deal as the kennels and equipment I left him with were worth a lot more than £500. It was a shame for Bobby in a way, he was lumbered with an arsehole who couldn't train white mice and it wasn't a good match. In the next two years I don't think they won more than a couple of races. I would have moved the dogs to Bill Dalrymple's there and then, but Bill was fond of my wife, and as it was obvious our marriage was falling apart I felt Bill thought I was the wrong one so the time wasn't right for what we would eventually achieve. Instead I leased some ground from British Rail, built another kennel and installed another old timer to assist me – Dick Finnie. Dick knew the game inside out but had no dogs, no kennel and no transport, so he jumped at the chance. We continued to turn out winners and I acquired another flying machine, Dins Rocket, who came second in the Derby but was disqualified. I also bought pups from a friend in Wallyford – John Bulcan. I had long had my eye on the pups as I thought they were real prospects. I got them because I did John a favour in his hour of need. His father took seriously ill and was at death's door. His brother was rushing back from Canada and was due to arrive at Prestwick at 3am on Christmas morning. John couldn't drive so I agreed to take him. I got him there and back with his brother in time to see their father before he passed away. I was still with my wife, just, and we went down to Wallyford for New Year's Eve with John, his wife Jean and their family. It turned out Jean was a cousin of Margaret Ormond, the St Johnstone manager Willie Ormond's wife. Willie and Margaret turned up as first foots during the night and Willie told us he had accepted the vacant Scotland manager's job that day, but it wasn't going to be announced until the Monday (this was Friday) owing to the holiday weekend. We dug deep, pooled our cash and, being a stranger, I was given the task of getting the cash on. Our tank was £400 and I went into Hills, Corals, Ladbrokes and a couple of independents. The papers actually had Willie as third favourite behind Sammy Baird and Dave Mackay so I asked for prices in that order, Baird was 6/4, Davie 3/1 and Willie 4/1. Split among all the shops, I got it all on at 4/1. Willie was duly announced the new boss and I went to collect our winnings. I was paid no problem by all except Ladbrokes.

I had two separate £50 bets with them and they claimed that there was a suspected information leak. They still had to pay out a couple of days later after we took our case to the ESBPA. Anyway, when the dust settled I ended up with two good young dogs and a few quid spare after paying for them.

While on the subject of Wallyford, there was another real greyhound man who was to become a good friend, Eddie Ramsay, who went on to buy and run Powderhall. Like Bill Dalrymple and I, Eddie put everything into his dogs' welfare and like us reaped the rewards. We had some ding-dong set-tos as our dogs were always well fancied and I think we finished about level pegging in all our clashes, which suited us both.

I said I would mention the Dundee Arms again. I was working with my bakery delivery van and every Saturday night I used to make a delivery to the pub, which was half way between my house and the bakery. When we came back in at night all our unsold goods were checked in then flung in the pig swell bin. There were all sorts of goodies: eclairs, strawberry tarts etc and the old bloke who dumped the returns was a greyhound man who won a few bob on our dogs so he let me help myself. I used to take bag loads up to the pub and it was hilarious. You have a pub full of burly draymen cursing, swearing and dragging their knuckles on the grounds and the next thing the shout goes up, 'Here's Alan,' and it was like a ladies' tea party with all the heavies piling into the cakes. Eventually they used to get their wives to wait for me outside the bakery and take their goodies home. There was nothing illegal and no money ever changed hands. The goods were fresh, they simply wouldn't last until Monday so it was better families got the benefit rather than the pigs. Could you imagine Sean Connery taking cream cakes home to his mum, but if he had still been living in Dundee Street it would have happened. What a pub that was. At one end of the street was the Co-operative milk depot and at the other end the Edinburgh and Dumfriesshire Dairy, both long gone. In our time Sean Connery had been a milkman with the Co-op and I was with the Dumfriesshire. The Co-op had stables and used horses and carts while the Dummy had floats. When Roy Rogers visited Edinburgh with Trigger, they were filmed in the Caledonian Hotel and Trigger was stabled with the milk floats in Dundee Street.

One other interesting thing about Tam Connery. If he hadn't become 007 he may well have become a professional footballer. He played right-half for Bonnyrigg Rose Juniors at the same time as Dave Mackay played the same position for next-door neighbours Newtongrange Star. It shows the calibre of the men and when you see what they both achieved … mind you the area at that time had some amazing names, with Dave Mackay and Sandy Jardine living within 600 yards of each other. Ralph Brand lived another 600 yards from Sandy and then the next scheme a short distance away had Graeme Souness, then close to him were Jimmy Murray and Jimmy Wardhough. Add the shops owned by Willie Bauld, Johnny Hamilton and Freddie Glidden with Tynecastle smack in the middle and you have one of God's chosen areas. Just for good measure, the sister of Chas Blythe, the paratrooper who rowed the Atlantic, ran the pub opposite the Connery's house!

My wife and I finally split up, although I was seeing someone else anyway and it turned out so was she. I fought her through the courts for custody of the kids but she won. She then turned to me outside court and said, 'You can have your brats'. Couldn't she have been sensible in the first place and saved all the lawyers' fees? This should have kicked off a happy new chapter in my life but how wrong can you be. The woman I left my wife for, Rosemary, was also married with a son and daughter. She left her husband with the daughter and came to live with me with her son. The idea was that when all was legally arranged for me to get my daughters we would all live together, but sadly her son developed a bone marrow disorder and died. She never really got over it and wouldn't entertain my family. I should have ended it there but I thought – wrongly – that maybe things would work out. I was self-employed by now so trying to run a business and look after three kids was going to be hard. At first all my friends helped out, looking after the kids for me, but it wasn't working and playing havoc with their schooling. The woman I was with, although we continued to see each other, got her own place for her and her daughter when she had access. My eldest two Lorna and Eileen were at school and the youngest Diane was only in nursery so I had to get a day carer in for her. Phil and Edith helped me out and the two eldest ones went to live with them midweek and they stayed with me at weekends. That couldn't last forever though and something permanent had to be done. My mother and her partner, who were both retired, stepped in and Lorna and Eileen stayed with them while Diane went back to live with her mother. They got the family allowance book, I gave them what was needed for the girls' clothing and upkeep. Things were reasonably stable. Although I wasn't living with Rosemary we still went out together and took our daughters on holidays. I took my girls twice on our own to Butlins and once to the South of France. While in France Liberation Day occurred. The bay at St Moritz was crowded with British and American warships, there were events and celebrations all over the shop, including a five-a-side football tournament. I got pally with a couple of Glasgow lads who were playing junior football back home at the time, and, with a couple of German lads we met in the campsite bar, we entered the tournament and lo and behold we won it.

My mother and her partner Alex were law abiding, taxpaying, upper-class citizens so imagine their horror one morning at 6am when the police came to the door looking for me. What had happened? I had been in Newcastle a fortnight before buying goods for my business. Although I locked the van I stupidly left bits and pieces in the glove compartment, including my single parent allowance book. Some yob broke in and stole the lot. When the police came to the door it was to say that a body had been fished from the River Tyne and it had my allowance book on it. My mother was up to high doh even though the police assured her it had nothing to do with me and they were only returning my property. She was finally convinced that if I had 'done him in' my allowance book wouldn't have been in his pocket. Mind you, had I caught the bastard he would have still ended up in the Tyne.

They lived in the stockbroker belt of town and Lorna's friends went to the world famous, mega expensive Mary Erskine Girls School. My mother and Alex decided this was where Lorna should go and I couldn't disagree because they had sent me to Heriots so my daughter deserved the same chance. Alex agreed to pay half the fees so Lorna went to Mary Erskine's. Luckily, Eileen had no such notions and settled for a new bike instead. Everything had worked out well until Eileen began bickering with my mother and the result was she came to live with me. I explained I had to go to work so she was the lady of the house, although she was only 12 years old. Things worked brilliantly, she learned to cook and made the tea every night and kept the house immaculately clean and tidy. She had started secondary school and I enrolled her at Tynecastle High. I dropped her off every morning and went to work, not realising I had a mischievous little minx on my hands. I had left something at home one day and came back around lunchtime to find Eileen and her pals playing their records, drinking cans of Coke and having a snack. To compound it, I got a visit from the truant officer confirming it wasn't a one-off, they were all regular offenders. Rightly or wrongly, I didn't do a thing about it except to tell Eileen to cut the truancy out, after all at that age I was as mischievous as anyone. How often she did or didn't play hooky thereafter I don't know, as I wasn't approached again until just before she was due to leave school when I was informed she and her pals had been at it again. Cheeky little devil said, 'So what? I only have two weeks left so it's not worth going back,' and that was it, nothing more was said by myself or the school authorities. She went to work almost immediately with the Inland Revenue and has been there ever since, steadily moving up the ladder. When she herself was eventually married and had two daughters thankfully they didn't develop their mother's bad habits.

With Eileen working and Lorna with my mother I was able to concentrate more on work. My business concerned buying and selling toys and fancy goods to supply to social clubs etc wrapped and named for their Christmas parties. Although only once a year, this was lucrative and it took all year canvassing. To supplement my income, I was able to take agency work or even a rep's job. I had two cracking jobs, one with a firm called Ray O Vac who were American and huge in the States. They produced most of the world's dry cell batteries, including Ever Ready batteries, and even equipment for the Apollo space missions. They decided to launch their brand in Britain and the pay was top of the range and the commission even better. I started off selling to the public via a van and every month they brought out a newsletter with a national league based on everyone's sales. Obviously in my first month I was bottom but then I moved up every month until I was top by a mile. Now this isn't boasting, the reason was the miners' strike brought about by Margaret Thatcher – the country was panic buying candles and dry cell batteries for their torches during the power cuts. I simply took the opportunity better than the rest.

I was helped though by the greyhound tracks. Despite the domestic difficulties, I still had my kennels and dogs and because of the power cuts the tracks were finding it hard to be sure of completing their evening meetings. Sure, the electricity board announced as far as possible areas and times power was due to be cut but couldn't be 100 per cent sure of their accuracy, and even at that if a meeting did go ahead the track lights had to be switched off between races and the bar lighting kept to a minimum. Here is where Ray O Vac came in. They had a square box which contained a battery about 9in long and 6in deep. Attached to that was a metal head containing a high voltage halogen lamp. This was a revolutionary gadget designed to rival the emergency lighting system in pubs and restaurants, which was costly, had to be regularly checked and was not always totally reliable. Ray O Vac's product cost a fraction of the price, didn't need maintaining and even had a carrying handle. They were also used in coal mines and since the mines weren't operating we had thousands of these lamps lying idle in the warehouse. Meanwhile, the tracks were forced to race in the afternoon, which was a financial disaster as the crowds were mainly working men who couldn't afford time off work, so gate, bar and tote takings fell. The McAlpines owned Wallyford and Wishaw, the Heffermans Armadale and Carfin, John O'Donnell Mount Vernon and several others I can't remember off hand, but they all bought the halogen lamps and the rest soon followed. They had to lay out between £3,000 and £5,000 depending on the track but it was money well spent as they were losing that in revenue anyway. They were used quite a few times so they paid their way, my dogs were very favourably handicapped and everyone was a winner due to Ray O Vac. I also sold the lamps to shops and homes and when the strike finally ended months later I arranged for all the lamps to be sold on to the mines at a reduced rate. As a result, my commission on my sales was astronomical. For about four months, until summer came along and lighting demand lessened, I was on £2,000 a week or more. I was offered an area manager's job covering Scotland, Northumberland, Cumbria, Yorkshire and Lancashire, my salary quadrupled and I was given a BMW company car. I was even more or less assured that when my boss retired I would replace him as General Manager UK. When I tell you what happened next you will think me mad, and you are probably right. I took the job but resigned a few months later. Bill Dalrymple had realised it took two to tango and Marilyn was as much to blame as I was for our divorce. I moved my dogs to his place at Dreghorn and it was the start of one of the most successful partnerships in greyhound racing. I gave the job my best shot but I was never 100 per cent happy. Most weeks I was away from Monday to Friday so I didn't really miss much dog racing as I caught the Monday card before I left and was back for Friday. Bill didn't mind the extra work but I still didn't think it fair. I didn't really like all the travelling and hated having the same conversation in a different hotel with different people every night. My other business came into it as well – though the fruits didn't come until the end of the year, canvassing still had to be done. I had met another great friend, who to this day still is, Wattie Nicholson, who could have and often did cover the clubs for me but I still wasn't really happy. With the friends I had I could have at a push run both jobs but I didn't want to. I didn't really lose out in the end because after concentrating on just the one business it grew and grew and, in the end, I was better off (although I didn't have a BMW).

The second cracking 'other job' I had was as an agent for a confectionery company based purely in Scotland so it fit in with my other activities nicely. It all ended in acrimony though. There was a dispute to the tune of over £800 in commission I was due and it dragged on and on. In the end I waited until I had a big week's takings, took my £800 and banked the rest of the cash for them. I left their car in a car park and posted their keys on with a receipt for my £800, which I thought kept it legal. No so. Not long after the police arrived at my door saying the firm were alleging theft. I had a pal, a Sergeant in the CID, and it was his boys investigating. I explained my side of the story and, though agreeing with me in theory, I was wrong in principle and they had to charge me and search my house. I told them they were wasting their time as I had 'done it in' at the bookies, a fact my independent bookie who was also a friend confirmed. He wasn't lying, I hadn't lost £800 that day, all he said was I had lost £800. Had he been asked to be specific he wouldn't have perjured himself but his statement was taken at face value. They searched the house and didn't find the £800 but found an envelope with £500 and a receipt in for a dog I had sold. They took this as evidence and even further searched my daughter's room and found £200. The wee devil had been saving her pocket money and housekeeping, and good luck to her. She hit the roof when she came home but I refunded her cash. Later when it came to court I was fined £30 but had the £500 and the £200 returned. Because I said I had lost their money it was deemed misappropriation of company funds and it was a civil matter for them to recover it. Because of all the aggro I sued them for my commission due, got it, plus expenses and they never bothered pursuing me, so I got paid twice.

The £800 dispute came in the craziest circumstances you could imagine. The company were based in London, so apart from the odd visit from the General Manager I was on my own, which suited me. The job was so simple, all I did was collect cash from the previous transaction and take new orders. Now one thing I can do is a fair shift. What I was expected to do in a week in Aberdeen I did in a day and a half. I went from Aberdeen right up to Inverness and back down again. Three weeks work which I could do in one, though I never told the company that. This General Manager was a real prat. With the time I saved I canvassed for new customers for the company and got 16 in one week. The canvassers for the company were paid £50 per customer so I was owed £800. The General Manager went ballistic, saying that's not your job and did we not go at it, with me getting the better saying if I can land 16 new accounts in one week it doesn't say much for you and your canvassers. As I said, it dragged on and on and I even took the matter up with the Chief Executive when I phoned him to tell him I had kept my £800, and he actually agreed with me in principle. I told him his General Manager was an idiot and I couldn't work with him so the car keys were in the post. He asked me to stay but I said only if you get rid of that clown, which they didn't so that was that.

I was now back to running my own business and the dogs. I went to the trade fair at Harrogate where I bought my toys, or at least ordered them for the following year. On my way home I was to call at the kennels in Pontefract to collect a pup I was owed for an unsatisfactory dog purchased earlier. I decided to go to the nightclub Cinderella Rockafellas in Leeds to kill a few hours, drive to Pontefract, park at the kennels and get a couple of hours of sleep before collecting the new dog first thing and getting back early to settle him in. I stayed in Cinderellas until about 2am. It was heaving as usual but all the ladies were together in twos and threes due to the Yorkshire Ripper still being at large. I left the club looking for signs for Pontefract, passing Leeds University and the ramp where the Ripper claimed his last victim. I saw a woman thumbing a lift and at first thought she was on the game and was going to drive on, but somehow she didn't look that type, and as I hadn't a clue where I was I stopped hoping to get directions. My first words were, 'Are you daft being out alone with a maniac killer on the loose?' She said she had got separated from her friends and was trying to get back to the Nursing Home where she lived. I told her I was trying to find Pontefract Road and she informed me the home was on that road so I said hop in. She said, 'Are you Scottish? What brings you to these parts?' and I told her about the trade show, killing time, going to pick up the dog and then home. Something clicked in my mind, I was the perfect gentleman and we made pleasant conversation. She was a Geordie and I told her about my times in Durham, and she told me she was training to be a nurse, and before we knew it we were at her destination. There was a long driveway before I could turn but she said, 'Just let me out here and I will walk the rest.' I did and bade her cheerio with the parting words, 'Take care and stay with your pals in future. We need all the nurses we can get, you all do a great job.' When I came back up the long drive, she was still at the top but with a walkie talkie to her ear and the penny dropped; she was an undercover policewoman.

On the way to Pontefract I crossed six roundabouts, all with at least two cars parked at the sides. She must have said, 'He isn't our man. He was completely courteous and concerned with my safety. He's had a drink but isn't under the influence. Make sure he is going where he says but leave him alone.' A few months later the Ripper was caught in much the same circumstances: a patrol car stopped him at random and his reign of terror was over.

I picked up my new dog, got home at midday and settled the new arrival in, never realising this was going to be the best greyhound I ever had or would have. A couple of weeks later Bill and I saw an ad in the Greyhound Owner for Clobast Rebel pups. We had always thought Clobast a genuine dog, early paced and a good stayer so I returned to Yorkshire to purchase a pup. The couple who bred the litter were Heather Garrison and her husband Jim, they were a smashing couple and we became friends. There were two dogs and three bitches in the litter; they intended keeping the bitches but the dogs were for sale at £500 each. I couldn't decide which one to buy as they both looked the part, and rather than pick one and find out later I had chosen wrongly I took the two for the reduced price of £800 for both. This turned out to be another great move. Before I came back Heather introduced me to Jack Moss, another dog man and an importer of digital watches which had just come on the market. I bought a stack of them and continued to do so until either everybody had one or the craze faded. Jack was a character, he lived in a ramshackle house next to his warehouse and dressed like Albert Steptoe. That was by day, he had a country mansion and dressed like a squire at night. The town house was a front to thwart the authorities. He lived in Thurnscoe and virtually owned the local track. The next time I went down I stayed with him and he flung a stack of Greyhound Registration papers and form history at me and said help yourself to what you fancy. He had over 100 dogs in various kennels. He just brought them willy nilly from Ireland and sold them as an agent for the Irish owners. I picked six out and the deal was I would train them, put £100 on the dog for him when it was ready for its first go then keep it or sell it and split the cash with him. We won first go with four of the six, the other two were no use and we found them good homes as pets. For pet lovers who hear alarming stories about greyhounds, you can rest easy here as far as Bill and I were concerned. We either raced our dogs until they retired then found them good homes or sold them to reliable owners to race on the licensed GRA track at Powderhall. In Powderhall the dogs were trained by trainers employed by the Greyhound Racing Association (GRA). The owner would be billed every month for his training fees or receive a cheque for his prize money less training fees.

Bill and I went to Powderhall every week if our own dogs were not running elsewhere, but we never had dogs in there ourselves, we preferred to train our own. To explain our set up, Bill was groundsman for the long-empty Dreghorn Barracks and had a tied cottage on the perimeter of the barracks. In the centre there was a 200-yard grassy hill which Bill manicured to track standard. We had our own drag hare and it was here at the base of the Pentland Hills that Bill and I formed a partnership that would be better described as a winner factory. I could write ten books about each dog but I will only highlight our major successes. The Clobast Rebel pups turned out as I thought and in their first trial on the track, a private trial at Wallyford, we pitted them against one of our fastest dogs, Lashing Time, who had been second in the Irish Derby. He was greased lightning from the traps, but on a winter straw and heavy going the pups slaughtered him, finishing within a length of each other. We thought we were nailed on for the puppy derby and I was asked by a local bookmaker to name my price for them but they were not for sale. You learn something new about dogs every day and you can make mistakes, no matter how good you think you are. I did both. The pups' kennel names were Wacker and Bond, their registered names Friendly Rebel and Forever Autumn. Wacker was down to run at Wallyford one night and the ground was hard and frosty. The handicapper assured me that extra straw had been laid and the ground was perfectly flat and safe underneath. I wasn't sure but ended up making the biggest mistake of my dog-training life. I ran him and he injured a toe. He was OK and won plenty of races afterwards but that injury at such an early stage of his racing made him wary and he never ever laid himself out as he could and should have, ruling him out of the puppy derby. Bond on the other hand was never injured and his early races went to plan. He was winning everywhere and as each month passed his times should have improved as he was still developing. They weren't and though he was winning I felt he wasn't laying himself out as he should have. Bill and I never took chances with our dogs' health, any doubts and we called the vet. Bond was declared as fit and healthy a dog as our vet had ever seen. To run in the puppy derby you had to be running at a registered track so we had to put them into Powderhall to qualify for entry. They both won their trials easily in good times and were put on the racing strength. Wacker injured a shoulder in his first race so we brought him home as he wouldn't have been fit in time for the derby. Bond won his first race at 5-2 favourite and qualified for a race sponsored by Willie Bissett, who as I mentioned earlier had helped get me started. Because his time was the slowest of the finalists he was given TPI and a price of 10-1. You are not supposed to but we sneaked him out of the kennels and gave him a bath and a gallop and then took him back without the trainer having any idea. He slept a mite in the final but his pace in the back straight made up lost ground and his finishing speed got him home by a neck. This was something else I was to learn, Bond won his next three races on the trot finding lengths in every race. The penny dropped. They had been kennelled together since we got them and Wacker had been bullying him. He didn't win the derby or even get near it and he was too exposed to run on the flapping circuit so I sold him to some Powderhall owners who kept him where he was happiest – in Powderhall. He was a great servant to them, winning many more races until he retired and lived as the family pet. I gave Wacker back to the Garrisons, whose kids adored him. Next up was Danny, or Greenare Missile as his registered name was, the dog I had picked up at Pontefract. From the time we got him he did nothing but improve and won on every track we ran him at, breaking three track records. A local bookmaker Kenny Waugh sponsored the Trades Handicap at Wallyford. We fed Danny every round to the final and left him short of work in every round, but he easily made up the final leaving us knowing we had lengths in hand. We gave him a good gallop on the drag hare the night before the race. We gave him a bath in the morning then shut him in for the rest of the day. His coat gleamed as he strutted round the pre-race parade like the champion he was, landing us the £800 first price, the richest ever run for a handicap at a flapping track. For good measure our other dog in the final finished third, winning another £150. £950 prize money and £400 at 7-2 was a good night's work. My pal Bobby Sinton was home on leave as he was still in the Army and watched Bill and I give Danny and our other finalist King their final gallop. I told him both were trained to the minute and, all things being equal and the race being trouble free, Danny would win. The bookies opened King at 5-2 and Danny at 7-2. I don't know why, probably because King had been running in Powderhall, but the owners weren't happy with their trainer and brought him to us. They stood beside Bobby, watched the gallop and took my advice and backed Danny with a small saver on King just in case. Bobby didn't listen, saw the public backing King and ploughed in on him. When he told me in the bar after the race I could not believe him. He actually thought we had put him away with our advice to bet on Danny. He had been privileged to see the dress rehearsal and ignored it. He even saw me bet on Danny and he still bet on the other dog, who Bill and I didn't even have a saver on just in case! Danny went on to win his next three races, open races at Falkirk and Armadale, then we gave him a long and well-deserved rest to ready him for the Christmas Handicap. Bill was an expert at guiding dogs to finals, giving them their meal before their race in the early rounds and leaving them just a touch short on work. I didn't always agree but he was the senior partner so I went along with him, but my belief was if you had a good mark in an early round and the price was decent, go for it. You were still in with a chance of winning the final and you were in pocket beforehand. The Christmas Handicap proved me right. Danny was off an unbelievable four yards in the first round, mainly because he had had a long rest and the handicapper thought he had been injured. He was a certainty even fed and a gallop short, but I only had £50 on him because he had been fed. He won easily and was pulled back to two yards for the next round. Bill did the same and he won again, but again I only had £50 on because he had been fed. He was pulled back to scratch for the semi-final and same story again: fed and only £50 on. This time though he met trouble and finished third but still qualified for the final. So here we are in the final having won two races, and we should have ploughed in on him but didn't, sitting off scratch, giving eight yards to a dog we were sitting level with in the first round. We did the same as last time, final gallop, bath, shut in and then the race. This time it didn't work, he was the shortest price he had been in the whole tournament, 6-4 favourite, with the toughest mark.

He was brilliant in defeat, losing by a short head after getting a slight bump at the first bend. You can't win them all but that was a sore one to lose. Danny stayed with us until he retired then lived as a pet in the house with Bill for the rest of his days. As I said, we were a winner factory but you never win them all. We were to enjoy four more years training together then one night, sitting in front of the fire after bedding the dogs down, we decided we had nothing more to prove. The game was getting harder, tracks were closing left, right and centre, there were fewer bookmakers attending making prices skimpier, and even Powderhall was in decline. The barracks were being opened again, restricting our gallops, and there was a Premier Inn going to be built next door. When the barracks opened the nearby ranges would be in use sounding like fireworks and upsetting the dogs. Our six superstars were at the veteran stage and ready to retire so we joined them.

To finish my greyhound tales let me tell animal lovers and anyone else concerned that the stories about cruelty aren't true. Yes, there are arseholes who think you can dope a dog to run faster or slower, but they are a minority and never last long in the game. A dog will do its best if it is trained properly and fed a proper healthy diet. Dope won't make them run faster, unlike an athlete they don't know what it's supposed to do. You can dope a dog to run slower but what's the point, you still have to get it to run faster again and you don't know how much damage you may have done. The only system we ever used was tried and proven. A quarter pound of fresh mince mixed with a quarter pound of shredded suet slowed a dog by seven lengths without affecting it in any way. It simply felt full and didn't want to run any faster than it wanted to. We only used that when we had a new unexposed dog. We would go around four or five tracks with the dog slowed for his or her first couple of runs. We would then rest them for a fortnight then go back and win at leisure with our seven lengths in hand. One trick I used to play was to suck a Smartie until it turned white and then give it to the dog, letting the punters wonder if it was to make it faster or slower. They never twigged.

Once you were exposed you trained them as normal and if you didn't fancy them you gave them their evening meal early, it wouldn't stop them but it gave you a little edge. We had some great times and if only they would talk they would say the same. Every dog we ever had was trained to the minute, fed on only the best meat and vegetables, given fresh eggs every morning, clean straw three times a week and every day in winter. Sometimes for a change of scenery we would take them down to a deserted beach early in the morning, give them a gallop then let them swim as the salt water was good for the joints. Here endeth the lesson on greyhounds.

My grandfather and grandmother McHardy.

Me at Trafalgar Square with my mum in the background.

The Burry Man. The kids followed him like the Pied Piper.

The Hawes Inn made famous in Robert Louis Stevenson's Kidnapped.

The good old ferry boats. I can't remember if the bloke on the quay had just missed the ferry or backed the last favourite and was thinking of jumping! The stretch between the quay and the bridge was where we hunted for coins and caught crabs at low tide.

Catherine Bank (white house in the centre) my home for the first 20 years of my life.

GEORGE HERIOT'S SCHOOL - 1955 - 56

The whole family.

My father with my daughters, Diane and Eileen.

*Canadian cousins
with Ian and Maire.*

Best pal ever, Jock.

Next best pal ever, Ben.

Elaine's parents, Netty and Pat.

66 Squadron team after the game was postponed, costing us the cup. Left to right: Smart, Kay, Slocombe, Higgins, Haynes, Blakemore, Hogan, Grogan, Finlay, Ramsay and Warner.

Me running the 5,000 metres for a cup.

Swimming in the River Wear in Germany.

Me and Elaine on our first date in Aberdeen over 35 years ago.

Elaine helps watch while I look for any artefacts 'not nailed down.'

Elaine and I in Arnhem while dealing with Quick Shorts. Notice the Galucci shirt as worn by Del Boy in Only Fools and Horses. I had the gear long before he did!

BURGERS ZOO ARNHEM

Elaine's 50th birthday.

Elaine and me with Alex in his Suite.

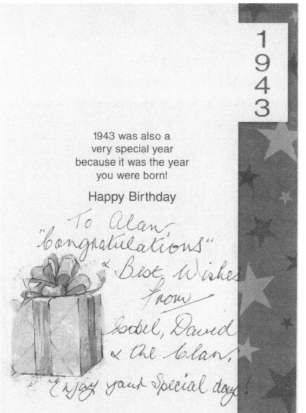

1
9
4
3

1943 was also a
very special year
because it was the year
you were born!

Happy Birthday

To Alan,
"Congratulations"
& Best Wishes
from
Isobel, David
& the Clan.
Enjoy your Special day!

My 50th card from Davy and his family.

Sad days, my dog racing partner Bill Dalrymple's funeral.

A Service of Thanksgiving to celebrate the life of

William Dalrymple
27th Oct 1923 – 17th Jan 2011

Mortonhall Crematorium
Wednesday 26th January 2011

With Alex Ferguson's Against the Grain, at Mark Johnstone's yard.

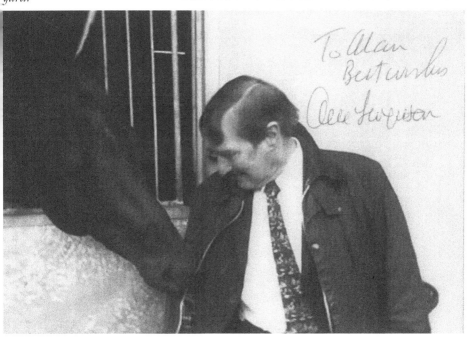

To Alan
Best wishes
Alex Ferguson

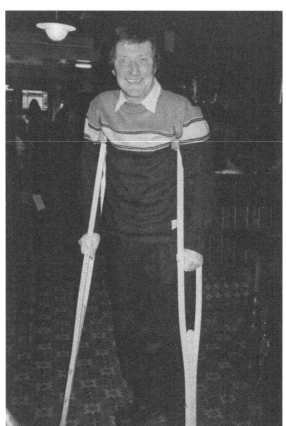

Me with a broken leg at Bernard Manning's show.

From John Macdonald's funeral.

The family thank you for your presence here today and invite you to join them for refreshments at the

The Raeburn Hotel
112 Raeburn Place
Edinburgh
EH4 1HG

There will be a retiral collection in aid of Cancer Research UK.

In loving memory of

John Macdonald

31st August 1944 - 25th February 2018

Thursday 8th March 2018, 1pm

Warriston Crematorium

Lorimer Chapel

Jim Stephenson and Denis Law at Davy's dinner.

Ron Cooper with Alan Short at Davy's dinner.

Ron Cooper and Martin Buchan at Davy's dinner.

The programme for Davy's last tribute.

Jim Stephenson, Alex and Jimmy Bouthrone with their good ladies.

On 25 August at Haydock. Middle second left is Harry Green, the ex-Blackpool, Newcastle and Scotland player.

Charlie and Kevin Boyd outside Old Trafford. Charlie (right) has been an enormous help in producing this book. They were nervous when they went to Old Trafford; being Hibs fans they were allergic to crowds!

Davy and me at his 70th birthday.

The Kate's Story Trophy won by Bond (Forever Autumn). We thought the Puppy Derby, Edinburgh Cup and Derby itself would follow, but sadly not.

The gang in the directors' box at Old Trafford. Left to right: Jimmy O'Donnell, Jock Macdonald, me, Eddie Cairns, Mark Johnston, Bobby Elliott, Andrew Elliott and Charlie Johnston.

Karl Smith in the seat Oswald was arrested in at the cinema.

Karl Smith in Dallas with Oswald's arresting officer.

With friends at Haydock.

CHAPTER FOUR

I am now 40 years old and from my boyhood days Jock Mcdonald, Jim O'Donnell, Bobby Sinton and Wallie Nicholson are still and always will be lifelong pals I would trust with my life. My business is going to boom. I am going to meet some of the most famous people around and what will be the two greatest loves of my life are about to enter the arena. I will meet up with my father again and keep in touch this time till he dies. I will get my second collie who will be the third love of my life and I will see my beloved Hearts win three cup finals.

I was working with a girl who knew the toy game inside out as her father had a wholesale warehouse. Everyone thought there was something in it but there wasn't. We were to meet the committee at the Navy Club and she asked if she could bring a pal along. When I saw her pal, a stunning blue-eyed slim blonde, it was love at first sight. Before I go on I will go back to our Palais days. There was a revolving stage, the big band would play for a while then the stage would revolve and the rock n' roll singer Shortie would come on with his group and a female singer, a stunning blonde whom every bloke in the Palais swooned over. Back to the present and that stunning blonde is the same stunning blonde I have just fallen for, Elaine Shelley. Believe it or not regarding women in those days I was a bit shy and certainly not the best chat up merchant. I went up to Elaine's house the next day intending to ask her out on our own but ended up asking her if she wanted to come to the PO's Mess at Rosyth that night. I supplied the mess with their fancy goods for their raffles. Elaine readily agreed to come with her pal. Elaine told me later that the said pal told her not to get any ideas about me so Elaine held back and stupid me thought so much of her I didn't want her to think I was pushing my luck. Anyway, the PO who dealt with buying from me stepped in first, they dated and married and I cursed my stupidity. Elaine's new husband Joe was an addicted slot machine gambler, fiddled the mess funds, was demoted to Killick and posted out. In the Army he would have been court-marshalled and kicked out, luckily as it turned out for me he was in the Navy. A while later he was given his rank bank, returned to Rosyth and unbelievably was reinstated as Mess Convener, which meant he was dealing with me again and I was back in touch with Elaine. There were no slip ups this time around. They were short of money due to Joe's addiction so Elaine had to get a job. She came to work for me, which was the joke of a lifetime. In our first week we went to Aberdeen and by the end of the week she didn't work for me, she was my partner in business and for the rest of our lives in every way.

Since that first night in Aberdeen there hasn't been a day when I haven't told her I love her and vice versa. She divorced Joe, I helped her get her first house and she moved in with her two boys, Malcolm and Derek. It wasn't plain sailing at first because Rosemary was still on the scene. Elaine resented it and rightly so, but Rosemary had enough on me to drop me in deep shit, and she tried to land Elaine in it but it didn't work. So I continued to see Rosemary until I annoyed her enough to dump me and that's when Elaine and I were comfortably able to move in together. Although she was history, I was sad to hear later that Rosemary had died from a brain tumour. I didn't hear about it until months after but I would have attended her funeral had I known.

Elaine and I were inseparable, I was her parents' ideal choice and I loved them to death, Netty and Pat. My father got in touch with me through some distant relatives in Queensferry and Elaine and I travelled down to Bolton to meet him. While we were sitting in the living room two bundles of sable fur came bursting in, my father's new wife Hannah's daughter's rough collies. One made straight for Elaine and me and as Elaine is a devout animal lover enter the third love of my life, Ben. As Hannah's daughter was a prison officer and didn't really have time to keep the pups it didn't take much persuading to get her to sell us Ben for what she had paid for him. My father and Hannah ended up keeping the other pup. Ben came home with us and what a great dog he was. Elaine and I were to travel up and down south a lot in the next year or two and when we could we would take Ben with us. Often when we were bringing an estate car full of goods back we would have to leave him with Pat and Netty. He hated it but put up with it, good wee soul that he was.

About this time I met and became friendly with the first of the many celebrities I will tell you about. I did a mail shot to all the Senior Clubs in Scotland about their kids' Christmas parties. Believe it or not I only got two replies, from Hearts and Rangers, and I was to supply their Christmas parties for years to come. Hearts had been relegated and their players' earnings had dropped so I suggested it would save them money if they did some of their Christmas shopping with me. They took me up on it and I became particularly friendly with Jim Jefferies and Frank Liddle; in fact, Frank sold some of my wares for me in Stirling where he lived. He eventually emigrated to Australia. When Jim retired he became an area manager for Legal and General before he started on his managerial career in football and Elaine took out all of our insurance policies with him. When he teamed up with Billy Brown their careers soared, although before joining Hearts and bringing us our first Scottish Cup in 40 years they were at Falkirk. Elaine and I had travelled to Holland to do a deal with a sports firm called Quick Sports. Their boots were excellent and Jim and Billy ordered them for the Falkirk squad. As I said earlier, the Dutch were tight as duck's arses and wouldn't release the boots until Falkirk's cheque was cleared, so Billy and I had to wait hours at the customs shed until they were released. Several of the Hearts players, including Henry Smith, wore them and whereas Quick should have capitalised on it and dished out free samples they maintained their stance of cash up front and no freebies. Henry and his wife, Lynn, Elaine and I became friends and they were and still are a smashing couple. Hearts played a game against an Italian side and smack in the middle of the Evening News was a near full-page photo of Henry and clear as day the Quick boots he was wearing. I urged Quick to send samples to Henry and the other players, but tight as usual they declined. I eventually got fed up with their attitude and stopped dealing with them.

Just after I closed the door on Quick another opportunity jumped up at me, and as well as an interesting story it is also a mystery. We were at the trade show in Birmingham when I heard that the UK agent for Kappa sportswear, an Italian company, was looking for sub-agents. I contacted him and got the agency for Scotland. I didn't realise at first that Kappa was about to challenge Nike and Adidas and the other top brands, although their portfolio was amazing. They supplied virtually every team in the Italian league and most other European leagues, they were into Formula One racing and international yachting. Their flagship was the USA Olympic squad and they also supplied the athletics teams from many other countries. If you look at the pictures of Carl Lewis winning his Olympic titles you will see he is wearing the Kappa logo. The agent's name as I recall was Sohan Khan and he was based in London. He sent me hundreds of samples and I got to work immediately, and with all my contacts I got a raft of orders. I was even on the verge of talking to Scottish senior clubs. I sent Sohan the orders, they were delivered and I was paid my commission by him, not by Kappa. The next thing we know we were asked to attend Kappa's AGM and the launch of next year's gear in a ski village called Sestriere in the mountains above Turin where Kappa was based. This was something else, most of the village was owned by Juventus who as well as Fiat was largely owned by Kappa, sharewise that is. It was the Juventus pre-season training camp and luxurious doesn't even begin to describe it. It was also a haunt for international playboys. The Kappa executives stayed in and the other reps/agents stayed in the ski hotel, a 300-bedroom work of art. It actually looked like Colditz with its back drop, a fantastic view looking down the mountain to Turin.

We had flown from London, changed at Frankfurt and landed in Turin and on arrival found the airline had lost the luggage belonging to Elaine, myself and the Spanish agents. They told us just to go into the village shops and buy what we needed until our luggage was found and brought to us. We were going to be in the resort for four days but as the airline reckoned they would have our luggage by the next day we bought a day's supply. This was some experience when we found the prices, for me a jacket was £200, trousers £100, shirt £50, tie £15, shoes £90, socks £10 and underpants £10. Elaine's and the Spanish lady's clothing was equally expensive and by the time we had clothed ourselves and bought our toiletries it wasn't far short of £1,000. When we eventually claimed our insurance they asked us if we wanted to keep the clothing and accept a partial amount of the claim or return the clothing and be paid in full. We didn't want the gear so they sent us our claim in full but never bothered to collect the gear we'd bought. It wasn't a big deal as to be honest the gear we had paid all that money for I wouldn't have given £100 for in a bric-a-brac shop back home.

It turned out to be four days of luxury. The new range of Kappa gear was impressive, as were the personalities and models who strutted it on the catwalk. All our expenses were covered by Kappa and they must have been considerable. Back home again there were more orders waiting for me, so I phoned Sohan with them. Start of mystery, no answer to the phone, no voice mail, nothing. I tried for days, even called the phone company but there was no fault, just no answer. I phoned Kappa and they seemed very icy, telling me Mr Khan no longer represented them. I asked my position, telling them I had sent orders to Sohan and asked would they be delivered as I had my customers to consider. They said they would get back to me but never did. I had only met Sohan at the trade fair and never been to his London premises. I asked a London-based rep I knew if he would check it out for me, which he did and said the place was deserted and none of the neighbouring businesses had seen any recent activity or any activity at all for that matter. That was it, no one, not even at the next trade fair, had seen nor heard from him. No one including me knew anything more about him other than his name and phone number. No other company reported any loss of goods to him; in fact, apart from Kappa no one even recollected dealing with him. Obviously, he had worked a scam on Kappa which was obviously why he had paid my commission instead of Kappa. I reckon he got my orders and his other sub agents' orders, had them delivered to his London address, invoiced the customers to his own account and then scarpered. This was confirmed when my customers all said they had indeed paid him direct. It was so well set up that apart from us meeting in Turin none of the sub-agents had a clue who the others were. I was left with a whole stack of samples, my commission paid in full and as I never heard from Kappa again I scored for the samples. I later heard Kappa had appointed a former Rangers player as their agent in Scotland and I would have been sick at losing such a potential bonanza had I not heard yet again from another source that they shot themselves in the foot. When the World Cup was played in Italy they channelled everything into the Italian stores and the rest of their customers outside Italy were left high and dry awaiting stock that couldn't and wouldn't come until well after the World Cup. We later spoke to the Spanish and German agents at another trade fair and they said they had ceased dealing with the company because of this.

To be honest Sohan was a decent bloke, from what I knew of him in the short time I knew him, so I hope he is well wherever he is. Between Kappa and Quick, what might have been. Quick in particular was a real disappointment. Their gear was as good, maybe even better, than their rivals, their boots were tried and tested by professionals in Scotland. They had a ball, the best I ever came across, and UEFA actually tried it and approved it in European ties. Elaine and I hired the function suite of the Scottish and Newcastle Brewers Social Club and put on a show of their gear. We invited all the amateur clubs in Edinburgh and District and had a huge turnout. We sold over 100 team kits that night, plus boots and over 200 balls. I had to pay them cash up front for the orders but got them within three days of payment and distributed them. I urged Quick to open a showroom in Scotland but to no avail. You just couldn't fathom them. They came to Britain, to the NEC, to display their range with the aim of getting set up in the UK and as I am led to believe I was the only serious client they attracted. I had it made for them, the junior teams would have followed the amateurs, then the lower divisions, and as Hearts and Falkirk already had players using their gear the seniors would have followed. Everything they did was unprofessional. They would pick us up at Schipol Airport and take us to the factory at Hengelo but after that everything was down to us, hotels, meals, the lot. The firm had been owned by a bloke who died, leaving everything to his wife, who appointed a Chief Executive and he was the problem. Either there was something between the widow and him or he intended to totally line his pocket. I did go above his head to the owner and she seemed an intelligent woman. I told her about the rewards that were awaiting her company and she seemed convinced but was overruled by her Chief Executive. It was a real mystery why they didn't cash in, and after dumping them I have never heard of their brand again, which was a real shame. They were good, or at least their gear was.

I was involved with a third major sports firm and this was the most unbelievable of all. The firm was the Tyneside-based Bukta, and Elaine and I visited their stand at the NEC show in Birmingham. At that time they were kit suppliers to Hearts and I think they may have also supplied Hibs at one time. To help you understand, way back then, and even now, replica shirts are cheap to produce, the material comes from the Far East. I was buying the Hearts shirts in at £6 and selling at £12, a huge mark-up but half of what the clubs were charging. Hearts were at an all-time low having been relegated and failed to come right back up, so their shirt sales were not anywhere near where they should have been. Christmas was approaching so I bought all Bukta's Hearts stock – they must have been in trouble as they only had a couple of thousand pieces. Anyway, the Hearts commercial director Robin Fry, who I was friendly with, approached me to try and get some of my stock as Hearts had none. He wasn't happy at the prices we were charging the public but that's business. Anyway, we sold all our stock plus other good sales simply because we were not exploiting Joe Public. When I placed another order with Bukta in the New Year they refused to supply us saying we were undercutting their other customers. Now tell me what sense does that make? They are getting their price. They only lasted a few months longer before going bust, so perhaps I landed lucky not getting supplied by them. That was three major sports companies that didn't work out so maybe I was a bogey to them. Bukta were the strangest of all, though. Obviously, they were in trouble so surely someone like me taking all their stock at the prices they quoted should have been a godsend and may even have saved them. As it was they went under, Hearts had to look for another kit supplier and the man in the street was the main loser. I never really got involved with replica kits again as I honestly didn't have the stomach for gross overcharging. It's now a massive business and the profits are gigantic but it wasn't for me.

Elaine and I bought a glass engraving machine from a firm based in Bath. We were to go to their factory for a crash course on its workings so we travelled to London and stayed with Bobby Sinton. We did our course on the Thursday then returned to London to spend the weekend with Bobby, and what a weekend it was. On the Friday morning we went to Brick Lane in Whitechapel. This was something to behold. It was crammed with sweat shops which made all the leather and suede jackets and coats sold in high street stores through the country. We bought a few items at incredible prices; for example, a leather jacket that would cost £800 in a high street store you could buy for £100 on Brick Lane. A £200 jacket would cost £50 and you could buy slight imperfects for £10. It was our intention to take a van down and bulk buy but what happened next had to be seen to be believed. We went into the Jack the Ripper pub, which had a betting shop next door, and put a bet on the races at Musselburgh of all places. I backed five of the six winners and we saw a dog running at Monmore dog track called Our Ben (we had left our Ben the collie at home with Elaine's parents). It couldn't be ignored so I had £100 on at 10-1 and boy oh boy he romped home. At the end of the day we won nearly £2,000 and we went to Wembley Dogs that night and won another £250. I took Elaine to Ascot the next day to see Desert Orchid run and we won another £500 on the day. We went on to Wembley Dogs again at night where I met one of the trainers we had dealings with in our training days, Ted Dixon. When Ted brought his dogs up from Wembley to Powderhall's Edinburgh Cup he kennelled them with us at Dreghorn. Ted had retired but his daughter had taken over and had a young dog in the last race, Stoneyhill Sweep, named after their Edinburgh Cup winner. They fancied him, we backed him and he won at 5-1. I also had a few previous winners so it was another bonanza. When we got back to Bobby's we piled all our money on the bed and when counted we had amassed over £5,000 in two days. We hired a van on Sunday morning from National Rental, meaning we could return it in Edinburgh instead of having to drive back to London. We went to Brick Lane and bulk bought leather and suede coats, jackets, trousers and skirts.

Things were going well, we had our trophies, fancy goods, sports goods, sublimation printing, glass engraving and now leather and suede items. As I said earlier, I was friendly with Jim Jeffries and Frank Liddle and it was the leather goods Frank sold in Stirling and a heavy shilling he made for us both. Although the toy game was dying, Hearts and Rangers still asked me to do their parties for them. I was getting good business from the Army and I took some of the kids of the people who were ordering from me to Ibrox to get a tour of the place. On one occasion I bumped into Ally McCoist and Paul Gascoigne. I knew Ally because I often used to see him with the late, great Davy Cooper and his dad at Hamilton Races. I had never met Paul Gascoigne but let me tell you this, what a man he was. He was absolutely brilliant with the kids, an absolute gentleman with a heart of gold. It is tragic how his life panned out but it could have been different. You will hear later how I was to become friendly with Alex Ferguson and his brother Martin – Alex wanted Paul when he was with Newcastle but he went to Spurs. Had Alex got him I am certain he would have kept him on the straight and narrow, but sadly he didn't and Paul was left at the mercy of the wrong company.

Another lifelong friend was to enter my world at this point, Jim Innes, a self-made millionaire from Fife. I met Jim when trying to sell my wares to him for his pubs and hotels, which I did and you will hear more of Jim later. You learn something new every day and Elaine and I hit on an idea with our sublimation system. We started making signs for hotels on metal. We would put the hotel's name and logo on any sign they wanted and it would last for life. For example, we would put the Blackpool Tower logo on either side of the top of the sign and the hotel's name in the middle then whatever they wanted underneath. This was a real winner – we started in Edinburgh and got business in every hotel we called on. We moved into Blackpool and that was the start of a 30-year romance. I sold to hotel after hotel and I loved the place and always have. Blackpool is like no other place on earth, it buys everything and sells everything and there is a saying that if you can't find an item in Blackpool then it hasn't been made. I have made many great friends in Blackpool, the main ones being Billy Hill, Martin Haines, Craig Anderson, Brian and Simon Taylor, Barry Young, Karl Smith and his family and Joe Pisaccini. As the years went on I would take a party down from Scotland every last weekend of the Illuminations and we would go to Old Trafford on the Saturday. Alex Ferguson got me our tickets and he would meet the lads before the game. I also took, and still take, the same crowd in July for Haydock Races. For the first few years we stayed at Joe's hotel, The Queens, which was owned by Pat Mancini, one of Blackpool's most famous ladies. After Pat's death and Joe's retirement, we switched to either The Parkhouse or The Doric, owned by the Taylor family. Anyone going to Blackpool, I would strongly recommend these two hotels, plus Barry Young's Lyndene. Barry was my first-ever customer in Blackpool and we are still dealing 30 years later, as I am with all my customers.

As time went on and we expanded I met more and more people and virtually travelled the entire north of England and Scotland. Our sales took us from Aberdeen to Bridlington on the East Coast and Ayr to Southport on the West Coast – some territory eh?

Events from now on may not necessarily be in order but they all tie in eventually. Elaine and I had gone to Cyprus on holiday in 1986 and came home early in September to find Hearts bottom of the league after their first four or five games. Wattie Nicholson and I went to Parkhead and saw them beat Celtic 2-1. We both agreed it was the best Hearts team since the days of Dave Mackay, Conn Bauld and Wardhaugh, the terrible trio, so we followed them every week and saw them go unbeaten until their last two disastrous games. While I would do cash in the bookies on the horses every Saturday I would back Hearts every week and was collecting at will. Alex McDonald and Sandy Jardine were in charge and I was still doing the Christmas party thanks to the secretary Les Porteous, while I was also supplying Les's pub and restaurant with engraved mirrors and glasses. After the Celtic game I checked their prices for the league and the cup and found they were 50-1 for both. I put £100 on each and a £20 double and £10 on each and a £5 double for Elaine. As the season neared its end they were odds on for the league and 6-4 for the Cup, so a massive pay day was coming. To win the league would be £5,100 and the same for the Cup while the double would pay £52,000. Elaine would win £510 for each single and £12,500 for her double. I was winning so much on them each week and the bonanza of the league was looming for sure, so I went to see Les and Wallace Mercer the chairman, who I also became friendly with, and said if the lads land the double I will give you both and all the players a leather coat or jacket and a jacket or skirt for the wives and if any relatives want to purchase the said items I will supply them at cost price. Les took me to see Alex and Sandy and they were delighted, who wouldn't look a gift horse in the mouth.

With three games to go, Aberdeen at Tynecastle, Clydebank at Tynecastle and Dundee at Dens Park, the league was a formality.

I went to Sandy and Alex and said you can have your leather gear now. I remember Sandy's words: 'Alan, it's not over till it's over.' I said even if the worst happens, which it won't, I have had so much pleasure and won so much backing you every week I would still be in pocket. They ordered their gear and I delivered in advance. The Aberdeen game was the first-ever televised match and I have often mentioned it to Alex Ferguson, who was Aberdeen's manager at the time. Anyway, the game ended 1-1 but Hearts should have won. They were 1-0 up and John Colhoun was clear through with the keeper to beat when Alex McLeish put a stranglehold on him and pulled him down inches outside the box, no penalty and McLeish wasn't even sent off. Worse was to follow when Aberdeen got a penalty they shouldn't have had and equalised. The ball struck Ian Jardine's hand and Willie Miller the Aberdeen captain immediately picked the ball up and put it on the spot. I was in the players' lounge after the game and Ian told me what really happened. Jim Bett the Aberdeen player had blatantly pulled the ball down with his hand onto Ian's arm so a free kick to Hearts turned into a penalty for Aberdeen and the two points that would have won the league were lost.

The next week they beat Clydebank 1-0 and people said that was where the league was lost as they should have won by more but they got the points that mattered. It was the next week at Dens Park that disaster struck. Everything was wrong. Several Hearts players were suffering from a bug so they should have asked for a postponement, the referee Bill Crombie was an Edinburgh man and a Hearts fan, and although he refereed impeccably he erred on the side of leniency for Dundee when he turned down a clear penalty for Hearts. With seven minutes to go and Hearts holding on, Albert Kidd nodded a cross towards goal. Wattie Kidd should have punched the ball out instead of his pathetic attempted header to clear it. Sure Dundee would have had a penalty and Kidd would have been sent off but they might have missed. Kidd shouldn't have even been playing as he had been injured and George Cowie had been brilliant in his absence. Anyway, Dundee scored again in the dying seconds and Celtic won 5-0 at St Mirren to kill the dream. On the morning of the game Hearts were unbackable and I had 50-1 and Celtic were 6-1. A bookmaker friend of mine said why don't you put £5,000 on Celtic, that way you are guaranteed £30,000 one way and £62,000 the other. I declined. Elaine begged me to cover her bet but I didn't do that either, because to get the full sum Hearts still had to beat Aberdeen in the Cup Final. Hearts had to have a seven-goal turnaround to lose the league and that seemed unthinkable, but it happened. Honestly who would have ever imagined it ending as it did; if the same situation arose 1,000 times over you would never get that result again. The next week was a formality for Aberdeen. Hearts were never going to lift themselves after Dens Park. Walter Kidd got skinned alive just before and just after half time and gifted the Dons two goals after John Robertson blasted over the bar for Hearts when it was easier to score, then Kidd got sent off leaving his team down to ten men. Alex McDonald said football is a funny old game, Sandy Jardine was convinced St Mirren had laid down to Celtic but, whatever, the dream was over and our city rivals were merrily singing 'You're forever blowing doubles', which we did. Wallace

Mercer the club chairman was gutted and so was Les Porteous, but they never forgot my gesture in honouring my promise in advance.

Elaine and I had been at a trade show and though we were not dealing much in toys anymore we spotted a new range of furry toys, the best we had ever seen, so we placed an order and sold them right away. I asked the company's rep to call in and see us for another order. We were needing a lot of storage space and needed somewhere bigger so I spoke to Wallace Mercer and he gave me one of the large cells, which the police had once used to hold miscreants arrested in the ground. I had to go to Glasgow so I left Elaine to deal with the rep. I told her to pick the lines she wanted and order a dozen of each. She selected the entire range, which was OK as they sold like hot cakes, but the devious shit of a rep altered the order to a gross of each, which we were not aware of until I got a call from Wallace saying there was a truck load of furry toys awaiting me outside the cells. Now I could have sent them back but I decided to teach the devious rep a lesson. I took the lot intending to take what we wanted and then tell the company to take the rest back. When I contacted the company I was told the rep had died of a heart attack and his records were in a mess. I instructed them to come and collect their goods but no one appeared. When weeks later they did appear Wallace told them I had moved out and he had no idea where I was. I never heard from them again so the devious rep did me a favour as I ended up with a buckshee load of goods. As I said, Elaine and I were friendly with Henry Smight and his wife, and Henry and I had a lot of fun in the close season doing beat the goalkeeper at local events. Henry continued to be a great servant to Hearts and Scotland, but the last chance of glory had gone, for now at least, at Dens Park. Wallace sold out to Chris Robinson's mob and though not the best outfit they did at least bring Jim Jeffries and Billy Brown back and after a 40-year wait they brought the Cup back in 1998 after beating Rangers 2-1 at Parkhead. Robinson sold out to Romanov's Lithuanian gangsters and though two more cup wins were registered the club was sinking fast until the present regime came to the rescue.

Elaine and I were regulars at Blackpool and on one visit I noticed an article about Jack Berry the horse trainer and his fundraising for injured jockeys. He had various events coming up and I offered crystal from our trophy range for prizes. He invited us to pop into his yard at Cockerham and he and his wife Jo and Elaine and I have been friends ever since. As things went along I began to keep a record of Jack's successes and on our sublimation system I made metal plates of all his winners. It was at this point I met another lifelong friend, Sam Hoatson, and his wife Rita. Sam and I went down to Cockerham and spent a couple of days putting the plates up that are made for him naming all his winners, and shortly after the Channel Four Racing Line team, while on their stable tours, admired our work. I composed a manuscript of Jack's career which we sold to fundraise for his injured jockeys campaign. Rather than rewrite it I will include it at the end of this book. Sam ran an entertainment business that featured filmed race nights, very popular at that time, and we organised two fundraising nights for Jack's charity. One was at Marco's Nightclub and one at Musselburgh Racecourse, and both were a great success, especially Sam's race night presentation. Shortly after meeting Jack, I formed a racing club – The Scotia Racing Club – and Jack leased us and trained for us a filly called Clan Scotia. The club at first was a great success, the filly's first four races reading 4, 3, 2, 1 with the win coming at Musselburgh. On our first outing we went to Doncaster's Lincoln meeting, staying in Blackpool. The Sunday Mail gave us good coverage with their racing columnist Alan Thomson writing as Joe Punter came along. The accommodation was pretty basic to be honest and we were in three separate small hotels, but after much muttering and kicking stones everybody eventually got on with it and we had a good time, but I still remember Alan's column in the Sunday Mail: 'Heavy going on the Golden Mile'.

Our members came from all over the country, the first ones to sign up being my lifelong pals Jock McDonald and his wife, Lennie Dodgson and his wife Sandra, Jimmy O'Donnell, Sam Hoatson, Jim Innes and his pal Melvin. We had two couples from Aberdeen and they went on the first trip to Doncaster; in fact, they went on every one. They were real characters. They arrived at the bus half cut and were well away when we stopped at Southwaite services. The two ladies were so well oiled the husbands hung them on the railings while they went to the toilet. We went to Doncaster and instead of doing a head count on the bus back I just said, 'Everybody here OK? Right driver, off we go.' We got back to the hotel and shortly after the Aberdeen wives came up and said where are our husbands. Christ, I had left them at Doncaster. Just then I got a call to go to reception. It was Jack asking if I had forgotten something. As Blackpool was on the way back to Cockerham Jack brought them back to the hotel. It never daunted the Aberdeen couples as they still came back.

That first trip for the racing club was a really exceptional one. My daughter Eileen and Elaine made rolls and I bought spirits and beers from the cash and carry and we ran a bar on the bus. We had a smashing old bloke with us, Stan, no one even knew his second name. Stan got legless, peed his pants and God knows what else. Typical of the company, Jock and his wife Jean, another gem of a lady, took old Stan under their wing and when we got to Blackpool went out and bought him new trousers and underwear. The measures that Elaine and Eileen handed out were generous to say the least. Everyone was three sheets to the wind when we arrived in Blackpool, but we still carried on partying until the small hours. Needless to say the hotel had karaoke and I was reminded in no uncertain terms by Elaine about my small mistake, which I will mention later. We were all to go to Doncaster the next day, where Jack had two winners so everybody won and we finished up at Jack's yard on the Sunday to see Clan Scotia.

Over the year the club ran we were to visit Doncaster again as well as Pontefract, Ayr, Hamilton twice and Musselburgh four times. What a great crowd, Jock and Jean, Elaine, Eileen, Liz Cairns and her pals and the Aberdonians never missed a trip. As well as the races, we had our visit to Bernard Manning's Embassy Club plus our weekends at Cockerham for Jack's open day, and I wish we could do it all again, but sadly it won't happen as at least seven of the regulars are no longer with us.

At the same time I contacted Chris Thornton, the secretary of the Middleham Trainers Association, and offered to put up the trophies at their open day. Chris invited us down to his yard, the famous Spigot Lodge, and we had a fabulous night with him and his wife Antonia, the daughter of the legendary Sam Hall, who had also trained at Spigot Lodge. I am not a whisky drinker usually, but I sunk a few that night as well as a few beers. We spent two or three days in Middleham and I met and became friends with Bobby Elliott, the assistant trainer to Mark Johnston. As well as being assistant to Mark, Bobby was still riding but about to retire; in fact, he had his last ride that time we were down and won it on Human TV. We are still good friends and I stayed with Bobby every time I was in Middleham on my own. The club lasted a season and we had fun, but after the filly won everyone thought they were going to be rich for life. They (each one) thought they owned the horse, they would pester Jack for information at the races and in the end I got fed up with the phone ringing day and night, will this horse or that of Jack's win, is it trying? As if a trainer would say he isn't trying. Jack used to tell them if you fancy it, back it. The Sunday Mail took over from us but they only lasted a year for the same reasons.

Whenever Jack raced in Scotland I would go, usually with Sam and Jim Innes and sometimes with Jock and his son. It was at one of these race days I was to realise a boyhood dream and not only meet but become close friends with my boyhood hero Dave Mackay. His brother-in-law John Dixon, another gem of a man, had been talking to some of our company and then Davy came over and joined him. We got on from the word go and we were to room share whenever we went away if John wasn't there. That first day I met him was just before one of Jack's charity nights so I invited him along and he readily agreed. Davy stayed in Burton Joyce but came home regularly to his other home in Whitecraigs, which he and his wife Isobel retained and was occupied by John. Every time he came home I would get the call, are we going racing, and we did with Jack supplying our badges. For about five years in a row, Davy, John, Sam, Jim Innes and myself would go to the Ayr Gold Cup meeting, staying over Thursday and Friday and coming home Saturday. A crowd from London organised a testimonial in Edinburgh's Sheraton Hotel and I made up a pictorial history of Davy's life, which we framed, and Alex Ferguson sent a signed Manchester United shirt. The comedian Happy Howden and myself did the auction and we raised a fair old sum. Sadly, the money the Londoners handed over was paltry; in fact, it was less than Happy and I raised at the auction. The same Londoners were to approach me later to do a race night as part of Charlie George's testimonial. Jock MacDonald came down with me and Sam supplied the films. Although we didn't charge them, they paid all our expenses and to be honest they could have done it cheaper hiring a local firm. I met Frank McLintock the ex-Arsenal captain and we had a good old yarn about Davy. I was to meet him again many years later in less pleasant circumstances. Davy's 50th wedding anniversary was coming up and I arranged with Joe Pisaccone for Davy and Isobale to have the best room in the Queens Hotel and he laid on flowers and a special dinner. On Davy's 70th birthday a crowd of us went down to Derby, where Davy was still revered as he won the championship for Derby County as a manager. Jock, Jim Stevenson (another great friend who you will hear more about), Eddie Cairns (who was soon to become my daughter Eileen's father in law), Jim Innes and a couple of others all travelled down and stayed at a Holiday Inn near the ground. Davy reserved seats in the Dave Mackay Lounge and we had a great day. Davy decided to stay on and go out on the town with us, and shared my room with me. Dave loved his glass of wine but he didn't have a great capacity for it so he ended up well on. Somehow Dave, Jim Stevenson and I got separated from the rest and made our own way back to the hotel. I had to half carry Davy and that was some job, he was solid as a rock. Davy said he knew a short cut across a railway line so away we went, then he decided he needed a pee in the middle. I said, 'Davy, for Christ's sake, we are in the middle of the main line to London.' 'Don't worry,' said the bold Davy, 'there are no trains at this time of the morning.' We hadn't gone 20 yards after Dave had finished when a London express thundered by. Davy said, 'Well I never, you learn something new every day.'

Anyway, back to the present and my daughter was about to be married to a lad called Stevie Cairns. All went well and I was able to give a few quid extra for their honeymoon when Jack's Mind Games won the Palace House at Newmarket and I doubled it with the 2,000 Guineas winner on the same card. I was to get on well with Stevie and his father Eddie. I ran another trip to Blackpool with the intention of going to Bernard Manning's Embassy Club in Manchester. Bernard was putting on a show for Jack's injured jockeys fund. Elaine, Stevie, Eileen's mother-in-law Liz and a couple of her pals and the rest of the crowd all travelled down. Jack had been injured in an accident that day, but we had a great time and Bernard took us into his private suite after the show. We became friends and I always met up with him when we were both in Blackpool. Eileen, Liz and her pals came on all our trips and Liz was a gem of a lady who sadly died a few years ago. Things moved along at a steady pace for a year or two, the trophy business was running down, we had opened a shop but our hearts weren't in shopkeeping and we closed it. The hotel business was booming and we also met a great bloke called Clive Edwards who imported jewellery from the Far East. We went to Jack's annual owners' party every first week in December and it was here I was to meet Alex Ferguson. Jack had just trained his first winner, Queensland Star, and he and his wife and some friends attended the party. Jack used to put a horseshoe with a string and balloon with the horse's name on it on each table. I showed Alex to his table and he invited us to join him. It was a great night. At that time Rupert Murdoch was attempting a takeover of Manchester United and there would be wholesale changes. I asked Alex how it would affect him and he simply said, 'Ach, if I don't like it I'll find another job.' Bobby Elliot had told me about two horses laid out for New Year's Day three weeks later and I told Alex about them and they duly won. Elaine had bought me my first mobile phone for Christmas and I was in Jim Jefferies's office at Tynecastle when my new phone rang and it was Alex saying, 'Well done my son.' Alex Ferguson and Jack Berry are two of the finest men I have ever met. Alex has been knighted and Jack given an MBE. It is my opinion it should be Sir Jack Berry and Lord Ferguson. Jack deserves it for his tireless charity work. With the players, Alex has made multi-millionaires, and he has made countless millions for the Treasury from their income tax. The year moved along, we moved into the Scarborough hotel scene and did well, and I covered all the hotels from Middleham in the Dales over to Blackpool, which meant I saw a lot more of Bobby. I went to Hamilton one day in July and cleaned up, Jack had three winners and Mark Johnston two and I backed them all. I decided to treat Elaine to a holiday in Turkey with my winnings and told her to book it, which she did paying cash. I mention cash because it has an unfortunate relevance to what is to follow. As Elaine was booking the holiday I took Ben to the vet as he had been unwell. I received the heartbreaking news that he had cancer and wouldn't get better. While in Middleham I had engraved some crystal glasses for Mark and Deirdre Johnston and became quite friendly with them. Mark was a qualified vet so I asked him for a second opinion. Although he couldn't cure Ben he at least gave him an extra nine months, telling me that as long as the dog was in no way distressed and walking and eating normally there was no immediate need to put him to sleep. Back to the cash. Elaine always paid by cheque but because I had given her cash she used it to pay for the Turkish holiday. No way were we leaving Ben so we decided to cancel. Had Elaine paid by cheque we could have stopped it. We did try and claim on the insurance, saying Elaine had slipped in the shower and injured her back. She did indeed have back trouble and we said the fall had aggravated it, but they refused our claim saying Elaine hadn't informed them she had a back problem. Tough luck but I would have done the same thing 100 times over, no way would we leave Ben. Beware insurance companies though.

I will go back a bit again and tell you about some great Glasgow people: Alan Short, Jimmy Aitken, Ron Cooper, Hugh O'Donnell and Willie Bennett. Much has been written about them in the press but compared to the likes of George Galloway and Tommy Sheridan passing as politicians, Fred Goodwin costing the bank's customers millions and all the crooked politicians fiddling their expenses, these guys are saints. I am and always will be close friends with them and would trust them implicitly no matter what. Sadly Ron Cooper died a few years ago but the rest are hale and hearty and long may they be. Before I moved into the hotel business in Blackpool, Glasgow was a godsend for us. Everywhere we went we got orders, and after Edinburgh it was Glasgow's hotels that got us set up in our signs business. From the Jaguar Club in Paisley Road we covered the bowling clubs and social clubs including the Rangers Social Club and Rangers themselves. There was a gap to the Red Lion and its neighbours, then Jim Baxter's pub. We then went on to London Road and got all the pubs around the Barrowland and Celtic Park, including the Celtic Social Club and Celtic themselves. We then got about a dozen hotels on Argyle Street plus Hugh O'Donnell's health clubs. It was through Hugh that I first met Jimmy Aitken and Ron Couper. That was amazing business and kept us so occupied that we didn't have time to canvass new customers, and this reveals an amazing story. As we canvassed originally and built up our custom, I had called three times at a pub called Fergie's but never got the owner in. The pub was owned by Alex Ferguson and in his first book he tells how you could buy anything there. Given the response we got in Glasgow it is odds on we would have done business. We sponsored the Govan Ladies Darts League and they had their annual presentation in the Grand Old Opry next door to Fergie's. It's amazing I was only yards away from dealing with someone I would meet years later when he was in the process of becoming the greatest manager in British football history. As I said, Glasgow was fantastic, which is why I have always had the greatest admiration for Glaswegians. We sold our toys, leather and suede, our sublimation t-shirts, polo shirts and sweat shirts, digital watches, jewellery and sublimation signs, sheets and towels to the hotel. The pub next to the Red Lion was a starting point for parts of the Orange Walk and we got great orders from them. I met Alan Short and Willie Bennett through Ron Couper and they were to put more business our way, so all in all Glasgow will never owe me a penny. At this time another amazing occurrence happened concerning Rangers. One day Elaine and I were in the Red Lion with the owner Hughie and his wife Aileen and the next morning back home the papers revealed Rangers had been sold to David Murray by the Lawrence family for a reported £6 million. There was no indication that Rangers were even for sale – the Albion and the Social Club alone would have been worth more than £6 million, never mind the stadium, players, and any other assets. Had anyone been aware of this deal – I can think of hundreds and more who could have raised that kind of cash and more if needed. I listen to comments from Rangers fans over the years and in general they seem to think that was the day Rangers' troubles started. As I write this we know they are recovering from total disaster and I for one hope they never see another dark day. You can take from that that if I wasn't a Hearts fan I would be a Rangers fan.

There was another dinner in Edinburgh for another great Hearts player, John Cumming. It was held in the Craigmillar Hearts Club and Dave Mackay, Jock McDonald, Eddie Cairns and myself attended. Alex sent a signed shirt and a fair sum was raised for a great player. Craigmillar is a rough area and taxis just won't go into it at night so we had to walk for miles after the do before we even sighted one. There was another London crowd of Spurs fans who played on Davy's fame. They asked me to book a venue as they intended to have another testimonial for Davy. I ended up doing all the organising, sold all the tickets and did the auction and raffle. Martin Ferguson had earlier had a charity night in Glasgow for the family cancer charity and Davy attended that, so Martin reciprocated and was at the top table with Davy. Another pal, Kenny Paton, supplied the comedian free of charge so all in all I figured Davy should have got over £5,000. It was more like £500 they handed him, it was a disgrace but what could you do, in hindsight I should have handed the ticket and auction money to Davy myself but you live and learn. We went to another dinner in Hamilton one night. It was in Alex Forsythe, the ex-Manchester United full-back's pub and function suite. It was something to do with Tommy Gemmill and Billy McNeill and the sprinter George McNeill were the main guests, at least until Davy appeared. Sam Hoatson had been given a table so he and I and his son and Davy and John Dixon went through. No matter where he went Davy was the centre of attention, and he never refused anyone and never charged for his services. When we went racing at Musselburgh we would go into the Sportsman Bar which was owned by Ralph Callaghan and Jackie McNamara. People were forever sending Davy drinks over and Davy would always buy them one back. I was working in Scarborough once when I got a call from Isobel asking, 'Where is David, Alan?' I had left Davy and John badges for the races and told Isobel this. It turned out as usual Davy just couldn't get away from his well-wishers. When Davy wrote his autobiography it was one of the greatest honours I have ever had when I was mentioned in his acknowledgements, along with Alex who wrote the foreword. Another priceless item I have come upon as I write this is something else I received from Davy. At the centenary of the FA they launched a set of stamps featuring Davy, Denis Law, George Best, Bobby Charlton and Gordon Banks, with one for each individual player. As I write I am looking at the franked envelope with Davy's first edition stamp. What's it worth? The world to me. One of Davy's saddest stories was the morning he arrived at Enfield Golf Club for a players' day out to find his friend John While had been killed on the course by lightning, and it could easily have been Davy as well. Davy told me he and John liked to arrive early to hit a few practice balls and usually arrived together. On the fateful day John arrived a bit earlier and went out on his own. It was a tragic loss to his family and football.

Davy told me about Scotland playing Austria at Hampden but the city was fogbound at lunchtime and the game looked certain to be cancelled. At this time Davy was quite friendly with the businessman Peter Williamson, who owned the Grafton Casino in Edinburgh's Tollcross. After Powderhall, just about every Edinburgh punter ended up there. Anyway, with the game in extreme doubt Davy decided to return to Edinburgh along with Denis Law, Jim Baxter, Johnny McLeod of Hibs and their pal Ronnie Shade the golfer. They made a beeline for the Grafton, where they downed the drinks and played cards all afternoon. Around six o'clock the fog started to lift and as the game looked like going ahead they had to rush back to Glasgow. Despite being half cut, Davy told me they all played out of their skins as Scotland hammered Austria. The Grafton days were brilliant and I must mention Peter's nephew Victor. He ran the betting shops as Victor Gold but his real name was Victor Brierly. A great bloke, a keen pigeon man and superb bookmaker, fair and honest. Victor was the independent who covered for me in the confectionery row I told you about. I knew Jim Baxter gave him race tickets a couple of times. He was an after-dinner speaker at functions for Jack and Davy when I did the auctions. Davy and he were big pals and he was very friendly with Jim Innes. He once had the pub opposite Fergie's in Paisley Road West and I met him there a couple of times. At this time we were at our absolute peak in the toy and fancy goods game and I was about to meet another infamous character. All over Scotland we had over 100 social clubs buying their Christmas party toys as well as every police force, every fire station and every Army and TA Regiment. I had my daughter Eileen and her pals wrapping toys every day and night for a couple of months beforehand, along with a few others. At 10p a present they got their Christmas expenses easily and I always paid them a bonus after it was all over. As well as the toys, I supplied the Army Sergeants' Messes with their prizes for the annual social highlight, the Christmas Ball. They sold raffle tickets all year and the prizes ranged from colour TVs to just about every appliance you could imagine. I was visiting Glencorse Barracks outside Edinburgh finalising their draw order with the RSM in the Sgts Mess. We were blethering in general about things when the Great Train Robbery came into the conversation. The RSM said I am surprised no one has ever tried to rob an Army pay roll, not realising that's exactly what would happen a week later. On pay day at Glencorse, the Admin Officer, a retired major, the Pay Sergeant and a driver would go to the bank in nearby Penicuik, draw the payroll then pay out on pay parade back at camp. On this particular day awaiting them when they left the bank was a corporal called Andy Walker who asked for a lift back to camp. Walker was with the Royal Scots stationed at Kirknewton on the other side of Edinburgh. He had been an instructor at Glencorse before returning to his regiment so was known to the pay detail and nothing untoward was thought about giving him a lift. On entering the vehicle, Walker pulled a Sterling sub machine gun from his holdall and instructed them to drive to a deserted location, Flotterstone, outside Penicuik where he murdered them and stole the payroll. What happened can only be conjecture but for sure the people in the Land Rover knew who he was so they were dead men and they must have known it. Perhaps the Major and Sergeant were thinking if they tackled him in the bank car park then stray shots may have killed innocent civilians so waited until they got into open country. Whatever happened, the Major and Sergeant were shot in the rear of the vehicle and the driver was executed at the side of the road. Civilian CID and military SIB knew it was an inside job because of the weapon used. They checked all the weapons signed out but Walker hadn't signed one out in the normal way. He signed what is called a G1098 form, which covers everything from a tank to a roll of toilet paper. He must have thought the authorities stupid; sooner or later they were going to check every form and find the G1098. His defence would have been it wasn't signed out for the ranges, it was for instructional purposes and I never drew any ammunition. How did he get the ammunition? Before being returned to his unit as unsuitable, he took recruits on the ranges for live firing. Every recruit is checked and has to declare he has no live rounds in his possession before leaving the ranges but no one checks the instructors. Walker must have been planning the robbery and murders as he pocketed the 9mm bullets needed for the job. After checking every weapon in Scottish Command and all the paperwork Walker was finally caught. The night he was arrested I was due to deliver the toys and fancy goods to the Sgts Mess and Corporals Mess but as the camp was swarming with Military SIB and civilian CID, the RSM asked me to deliver the next day, which I did. Walker was later involved in a riot in Peterhead Prison which was broken up by the SAS, and you can imagine their reaction when they found out one of the rioters was someone who had killed some of his own. As well as brutal, the robbery was senseless. The sum stolen was £20,000, a lot of money, but Walker would have earned that in wages in three or four years. Had he finished his service and collected his pension and gratuity in the time he's been inside he would have quadrupled the sum stolen.

While at the NEC in Birmingham we purchased one of our best ever buys, a sublimation printing system. This printed logos and whatever was requested on garments and metal, and unlike the soon to be out of date screen print system it never washed out and covered thousands of angles screen print didn't. We were now able to sell amateur teams their team kit and print sponsors' logos and numbers on their shirts. I was also the first person to come up with the idea of putting team crests on shorts and socks. Everyone does it now but I assure you I was the first.

There has been so much alleged corruption at FIFA in recent years, involving Sepp Blatter, Michel Platini and Jack Walker, and talk of vote rigging for World Cups and God knows what else. My opinion for what it's worth is that Alex Ferguson, Martin Ferguson, Dave Mackay, Martin Buchan and Pat Crerand should have been nominated years ago to govern European and world football. Alright, Alex probably wouldn't have considered it as he was too busy putting Manchester United at the pinnacle but the rest would have been ideal – honest, no nonsense men who knew the game inside out. Martin Ferguson travelled the world scouting for Alex so there wasn't much he didn't know, Davy Mackay had won an English title and countless Middle East honours and was reckoned to be one of the greatest players ever, certainly different class to Platini. Martin Buchan is the only man to captain a cup-winning side on both sides of the Border so his leadership skills are obvious and he works for the Football

Association. Pat Crerand is a European Cup winner and a multi cap international and he works for MUTV as a presenter so he knows the media side of it. It will never happen but what a team they would have made, and all Scotsmen too you will note. I had always admired Martin Buchan both in his days at Aberdeen and at Manchester United and it gave me the greatest of pleasure when I met him one night in Alex's suite after a match. We became friends and he came over to meet the lads at Blackpool a couple of times, once being when we had a tribute night for him.

Another celebrity was to appear on the horizon, none other than Hollywood star Robert Duval who was directing a film called A Shot at Glory. My pal Jim Innes at this time owned Dumbarton FC and the film was to be shot in part at their ground. Ally McCoist was to feature in it. I was on my way back from St Andrews when I got a call from Robert Duval asking if Alex Ferguson would be interested in the film. I passed his message on and that was all I could do. The film was eventually released but it wasn't a great success and Alex definitely did the right thing not getting involved.

Also around this time came an unsavoury incident involving Celtic. We were doing a roaring trade for pubs and clubs with our glass-engraving machine and we did some mirrors for both Rangers and Celtic. We had no problems at Ibrox but at Parkhead it was like the days of the biscuit tin boys again, getting paid was like drawing teeth. The club were only hours from oblivion when Fergus McCann stepped in and saved the club and everyone got paid – including us. It's hard to believe a club like Celtic would ever be in that position, but worse was to follow at Rangers in recent years. When David Murray sold the club to Craig Whyte for £1 and people like Charles Green and Mike Ashley got their claws into Rangers, the scene looked bleak. Thankfully, Dave King and his consortium have now stepped in and hopefully they will steer the good ship Rangers back to calmer waters. As I have always said, though, you cross a Glaswegian at your peril and when word got out a few years ago that Craig Whyte was staying at the Balmoral Hotel I know for a fact a group of Rangers fans headed to the hotel to confront him. Luckily for him he had gone by the time they got there. One day for sure he will get his comeuppance.

Mind you owning a football club can be a precarious occupation and I will tell you some true stories. Alex Ferguson once asked me if I wanted to know how to become a millionaire – 'Bloody right I do,' I replied. He said, 'it's simple, start off a billionaire and buy a football club.' My great friends Jim and Anne Stevenson have put thousands of hours into their beloved East Fife for little thanks or reward. Jim Innes kept Dumbarton afloat for years with no thanks and when he tried to save Airdrie he was vilified by their fans, who wanted Stevie Archibald's consortium, and didn't they regret it when he did take control. When I say Jim and Anne got no thanks they actually did, but from an unexpected source. Jimmy Bonthrone had been a legend with East Fife and went on to manage Aberdeen in the days before Alex Ferguson. When Jimmy took ill Jim and Anne looked out for him faithfully. As Alex admired and respected Jimmy Bonthrone he admired and respected Jim and Anne for their kindness and has often met them. Manchester United had a hectic three games in a 12-day spell and Alex took the team racing to Catterick for a break. Jim Innes, Sam Hoatson and his grandson Bobby Elliott and his son (now a fully fledged jockey) and myself went to the meeting and went up to Alex's suite.

One of Scotland's top bookmakers Alex Farquahar was standing that day and I mentioned the Manchester United lads were there. Alex said tell them to be with me and I will guarantee them the best odds available in the country on each race. I told Roy Keane and he said great, so I introduced him to Alex and he saw the lads right. Regardless of what you read, I thought Roy was a great bloke. We had a good day but were a bit unlucky. Alan Berry had a horse running, Carlisle Banditos, who we really fancied. He led everywhere bar the line when he was caught, we had backed him each way so won a little as he was a good price. Tony McCoy gave us two pieces of advice. – One horse he fancied finished second and another one he didn't fancy finished second again at 16-1. We lost cash on the first one and would have won backing the second on EW but we didn't as we were told not to. That's jockeys for you!

On returning from Catterick, Elaine greeted me with the news I had dreaded for months. Ben was failing, so sadly another massive heartbreak when I had to put him to sleep. I vowed I would never have another dog but Elaine loved pets and a few years later persuaded me to get another dog. Enter the best pal I ever had, my Border Collie Jock, but plenty more about him as I go on.

The next month Jim Innes, Jock McDonald, Eddie Cairns, Jimmy O'Donnell, Jim Stevenson and myself went to Blackpool for the weekend, taking in the Manchester United game. We were to do this every year for the next 14 years. Davy Mackay became a regular and loved it, he was really just one of the boys. Mark Johnston and Bobby Elliott and their sons joined in and Jack Berry came a few times. The second year we went down was particularly sad for Jock and me as our great pal Jimmy O'Donnell had been diagnosed with cancer and that was to be his last trip. Alex gave us his and Cathy's seats in the directors' box. That year Davy took one seat and Jim O'Donnell the other. Shortly after Jimmy went into decline and on our last visit to the hospital before he died he held my hand and said, 'Thanks Alan, I have followed you all my life and never thought it would end with me sitting in Alex Ferguson's seat, even Rigsby couldn't get me that!' By referring to Rigsby he meant the financial boss of the local Hewlett Packard factory (Jim was the social club manager). Hewlett Packard were sponsors of Spurs at that time but Rigsby couldn't do for Jimmy what Alex and I did. Eddie and Jock had to turn away, but I couldn't and wouldn't as Jimmy had my hand and I am not ashamed to say I couldn't stop the tears flowing. What a guy and what a loss.

Exactly a year later at Blackpool again for the game, we were all together in the bar when I proposed a toast to an absent friend and again not a dry eye. Davy loved the lads and they him and he told them story after story about his playing days and answered all their questions. Davy only spoke badly about two people in his whole life. When asked the question, 'Who broke your leg?' his reply was always, 'I didn't break it, [Manchester United's] Noel Cantwell did.' This was a bit unfair, it was an accident and I don't think a free kick was even given. The second time was recorded in what is now a world-famous picture with Davy holding Billy Bremner by the scruff of the neck. In his autobiography Bremner says he accidentally tackled Davy on his bad leg, which had been broken a second time, and it was also Davy's first game back. Not so, and Davy never swore much but he told me, 'The dirty little bastard went for me deliberately.' He also vilified the rest of that Leeds team saying they were the dirtiest side he ever played against.

Around this time Davy phoned to tell me about a talented coach Rene Meulensteen who had worked for him in the Middle East. He wondered if Alex Ferguson would be interested in him. I phoned Alex and he told me to tell Davy to call him. I never gave out Alex's number to anyone but he said give it to Davy. Davy called, Rene got a job in the academy and worked his way up to first-team coach. The moral of this story? Had anyone else but Davy asked me I wouldn't have bothered Alex, and Rene probably wouldn't have ended up at Old Trafford. The next game we were at, Rene came to see Davy and the rest of us and Davy introduced me. Remember I told you how tight the Dutch were? Rene said let me get you and the lads a drink, you get their order, pay it and I will square it up. He buggered off and we never saw him again and I was £57.48 out of pocket. He will be mentioned once more and again it won't be complimentary.

I was a regular at Blackpool now every second or third week as the hotel business was booming and I was developing some great friends who would eventually come to the games and Haydock Races with us regularly. Elaine and I were soon to reach 25 years together and we celebrated with all our friends at Haydock's Thistle Hotel. The general manager was a friend of Alex's and way before our anniversary Alex's secretary Lyn Laffin, another gem of a lady, phoned me and asked me to call him. It turned out he was more of a rugby fan and as I had plenty of rugby contacts with being at Heriots he asked if I could get him rugby tickets, which I did regularly. He would swap his season tickets at Old Trafford for rugby tickets to whoever I got to supply him. Before we went to Haydock he would reserve us a room and put on champagne and sandwiches etc and he laid on a superb meal for our anniversary. We had to pay of course but the price considering the class of the hotel was cheap to the extreme.

As well as in Blackpool, I was building up the hotel business on the other coast going as far as Bridlington and it was on one of these trips that my collie Jock saved my life. Firstly I will tell you how I got Jock because the lady who gave him to me deserves to know how grateful I will be to her forever. Her name is Sarah Cousins and she has a stable in Lockerbie. She is the granddaughter of the great trainer Eric Cousins. We were introduced by Jack Berry, who had retired and moved back to Yorkshire to a village called Hunton where he bought and developed a magnificent country house. He had a dovecot but with no pigeons. Sarah had a loft full of a rare type of pigeon and Jack had arranged for me to pick up a couple of pairs and take them over on my next visit. I mentioned I was looking for a collie pup and Sarah got me one. Elaine and I were in Blackpool and we picked him up at Lockerbie on the way home. There he was, a wee 12-week old bundle of fluff, sitting in a huge horse box. Thanks Sarah, you don't know the pleasure he gave us. Anyway, back to saving my life. When you bypass Middlesbrough and climb a steep hill there is a parking spot before you cross the North Yorkshire Moors into Whitby. I used to park there and let Jock gallop over the moor. It was rough high bushes on one side of a track and trees on the other. Suddenly the biggest stag you ever saw with massive antlers burst out of the bush heading straight at me. I couldn't get out of the way in time and if he had hit me it's pretty certain he would have killed me. In a flash Jock was snapping at his hooves and drove him away from me into the trees. I was now worried Jock would get trampled but he soon came back wagging his tail with what I would swear was a smile on his face. From then on I reckon we covered nearly 20,000 miles in our time together galloping on beaches, which he loved; in fact, he was on more beaches than the Allies in World War Two!

I remember another night we had for Jack around that time for his injured jockeys appeal and it was a great night, with Jack and Davy supplying superb after-dinner entertainment. It was the weekend of George Best's funeral and we all went up to Alex's suite after the game. Mark Johnston and his boys came over from Middleham and we had a great time. We had a photo taken of Mark, Jack, Davy, Alex and me and I am sorry to say I have lost it somewhere down the line. There was another brilliant night around then when once again up in Alex's suite I met the Irish Prime Minister Bertie Ahern and his secretary/companion Bernadette. I got on great with Bertie but Bernadette and Elaine really hit it off – so much so that she decided she and Bertie were coming back to Blackpool with us. The Irish security people went ballistic and got their way in the end, but only just. Bertie was to come over himself later with some of his pals and also two other leading lights in the Irish Parliament. I have told you the high regard I have always held Glaswegians and Irishmen in, and I could write another book about the great people you are about to meet, but a couple of chapters will have to suffice.

CHAPTER FIVE

It was on another Blackpool/Old Trafford weekend that another great friend Kieran Coughlan came over from Cork with his partner Claire and their whole family, about 15 in all. Kieran and Claire had horses with Mark and that was how I met them. I arranged for them to meet Alex and they were delighted. What a marvellous crowd they were, and every time their horses ran they would come over and Elaine and I were always invited into their company. More courteous and kind-hearted people you couldn't hope to meet. On the next trip David Connor brought two of Bertie's team plus a master craftsman Dave Forde – the two MPs were Brian Cowen and Bill O'Keefe. Dave Forde presented Alex with a handcrafted Cork chair which was a real work of art, and much appreciated. Again they came in their droves, 20 of them. I laid on a raffle and they bought tickets like confetti. We were short on accommodation that weekend and we had to use three smaller hotels/B&Bs. I wanted to put the MPs in a big hotel but they wouldn't hear of it, they wanted to be with the lads. They stayed with Linda Easson at the Halifax Hotel and Terry and Lisa Cook at their B&B. Linda has welcomed us on many occasions and I can recommend her hotel to anyone visiting Blackpool. Terry and Lisa used to watch Jock for me if I went for a pint and we will always be grateful to them for their kindness. Once again what a time we had, you can't beat the Irish craic. They even had their priest with them and he was dancing and boozing with the best of 'em. You just could not believe how laid back they were.

They were to come over many more times and along with my usual crowd I honestly felt humble to know that so many were prepared to turn up when I beckoned. I told you I might not have been the luckiest gambler alive, but boy oh boy did the cards fall right when it came to friends. The Glaswegians were not to be denied and one midweek Jimmy and Ron Cooper from Glasgow, Donny McIntyre from Ayr (whose hotel we stayed at when we went to the Gold Cup), Jock McDonald, Dave Mackay and myself went down to the United v Arsenal game. It was Ron's birthday and as he was an Arsenal fan I gave him and Davy Alex's seats. Arsenal won and clinched the league, much to Ron's delight. The trip started with me and Jock picking Davy up at his house in Whitecraigs, driving to Lockerbie, parking my car and travelling on in Donny's, who was waiting for us at Lockerbie. We travelled to the Hilton in Manchester where we met up with Jimmy and Ron before the game. Early next morning Davy, Jock, Donny and myself travelled on to London to the Marriot hotel for Bobby Smith's testimonial. When I was in the Army I played against Bobby when he was with Aldershot after his Spurs days. He recognised me and we had a great blether about the bruises we dished out to each other; Bobby could dish it out but so could I and we had a rare old reminisce. When we arrived around midday there must have been around 200 Spurs fans milling around outside the hotel. When they spotted Davy they didn't half divebomb him. Davy and I were sharing a room so when Davy finished signing autographs we dumped our gear in our room and headed for the nearest pub and bookies. Davy was mobbed again and we had to go half a mile down the road to get peace, and even then he was in demand. It was a great night and our table consisted of Davy, Tommy Docherty, Steve Archibald, Alfie Conn Jnr, Frank McLintock, Jock, Donny and myself. As the night went on Spurs player after Spurs player would come over to talk to Davy. Our hotel expenses were paid by the organisers (the same lot who organised Davy's Edinburgh do) but Jock and Donny got the shock of their lives when they went to pay their bill. The receptionist said, '£150 sir. Each.' Before we left Davy handed me £200, half his fee, which he had refused but they insisted. I said, 'Davy, that's yours.' 'No,' he said, '50/50, you've done all the driving and paid the petrol, I want to pay my share and I've had a marvellous time, thank you.' We weren't finished yet though, we drove back to Lockerbie, picked up my car and went to Musselburgh Races where we won a few bob, not a lot but enough to end our journey on a fine note.

We were now regulars every last weekend of the Lights at Blackpool and going to the match on a Saturday and this is where we became friends with the boss of the Premier Inn beside the ground. His name is Vince Ward and he looks after us brilliantly, as he does all his staff every year. We were to have the night of all nights in the hotel later in the story. Another man who deserves a mention at this point is Damian Hilton who controls the hotel's parking. Not only does Damian reserve our places every year, he looks after the lads if they ever go on other occasions.

Elaine's father Pat sadly died and as her mother Netty wasn't well she came to stay with us. With this in mind and the business well established, Elaine stopped travelling so much and stayed at home to watch her mum. When Netty sadly died Elaine went to work at the Bank of Scotland in the IT department. She had spent years travelling all over and though we were by no means old crocks we were not getting any younger, and Jock was travelling everywhere with me anyway. But we still both went regularly to Blackpool with our friends Wattie and Anne Nicholson. She also developed a taste for the bingo at the time and I was in the local pub of my daughter's father-in-law Eddie when she phoned me and said I've had a little win on the bingo. 'Oh,' I said, 'how much?' She had only gone and won the national prize of £20,000.

Elaine and I also went to Bolton regularly to see my father and stepmother and we had some great times. I took my dad to Bolton dog track as I knew the handicapper, who had been handicapper previously at my local track Wallyford. We took them to Haydock a few times and although they said it was fun they weren't really gambling or racing people. We had a lot of good times with them but nothing lasts forever. Firstly, my father died and a year later my stepmother followed him and her funeral was the last time we were in Bolton.

On the racing front, Jack Berry had announced his retirement, handing over the reins to his son Alan. I honestly thought that Alan would be an even better trainer than his dad, but circumstances were to prevent that. Jack had built up a huge army of owners that normally Alan would have inherited, but they were all getting on in years and cutting back their racing activities. As a result Alan really had to do it all over again, which was a near impossible task considering more people were going out of racing than coming in. I see Alan regularly and I wish he was given the ammunition because, like his dad, he can train winners.

It was the millennium now and on the first day of the new century Alan took over at Cockerham. Looking back on it I was busy supplying millennium novelties etc to the hotels. All in all I never thought the millennium was a big deal and really, after all was said and done, it was only another Hogmanay. Maybe that's the cynical side of me because it was the same when the Forth Bridge had its centenary. Jock and all my boyhood pals and other 100,000 others lined the streets and banks of the Forth as Prince Charles did the honours. As I said to the lads, it's just a lump of steel, what's the big deal? Remember for the first 18 years of my life it was just about the first thing I saw every morning. Mind you I didn't half slip up. The promenade was crowded with stalls and their vendors selling Bridge centenary souvenirs and we could have made a fortune in t-shirts. As it was, Elaine and I spent the night with Wattie and Anne in their club back in Edinburgh, where as I remember we spent the millennium as well. I remember thinking that night, here we are on the last night of the century, if only the world had stopped for a minute and thought about what we had done over the last 100 years. Two world wars costing over 100 million lives, unspeakable horrors in the German concentration camps, ethnic cleansing, dictators and despots murdering their own en masse, genocide in Africa and the once beautiful country of Yugoslavia torn apart, assassinations, greed, corruption as never before, scandal after scandal. We could have and should have said let's not make the same mistakes again in the next century, but fat chance.

Just before the millennium had been Alex Ferguson's testimonial year and it was the year they won the treble. His dinner was held in Manchester at the G-Mex Centre. Elaine and I – and another couple of friends Sandy McArthur and his wife Ina – travelled first to Middleham where Elaine and I stayed with Brian and Val Palmer. It was to be announced in the Racing Post the next day, but we got the story that night, that Mark Johnston was buying Brian's share in the business. It was all amicable. Brian had helped Mark set up when he came to Middleham and it was always agreed when the time was right Mark would go it alone, and this was the time. Brian was a remarkable businessman. He had built up a highly successful company, Hinari, sold it for a fortune and built another company again.

The weekend started great; we stopped at a betting shop in Biggar and had a big bet on an Alan Berry winner so the weekend was paid for. Brian and Val, Mark and his wife Deirdre, Sandy and Ina and Elaine and I had dinner that night in Leyburn and were up early next morning to head for Haydock races and then the dinner. My phone rang – it was Alex Ferguson asking about Mark's two horses that were running at Haydock. They were both fancied and in the event one won and the other was second. Alex also had a runner that day but he said the trainer Oliver Sherwood didn't fancy it, it was only having a much-needed run to bring it on for a later race. It led from the start to the finish and won by 20 lengths at 20-1. Needless to say we were all furious, most of all Alex. All his family and friends were down for his dinner, his horse wins at 20-1 and no one had a penny on him. Alex was not amused I can tell you.

Brian came to Old Trafford a few times and on Jim O'Donnell's last trip he booked a table in the Lancashire Cricket Club and bought us all lunch before the game. Alex had another event later at Haydock and again I booked a table. Jim Innes and myself went down and all my Blackpool pals came as well. There were hundreds in the function suite and the treble trophies were on display. A piper played Alex up the stairs into the suite. Our table was the very first at the top of the stairs. Alex stopped and said, 'Hi Alan, fancy anything today?' He shook all our hands and continued on to the top table – what a man! The day itself was great, though now retired Jack and Jo were there and Alan had one of Alex's horses running. It finished second but all in all I think everyone either broke even or won.

My pal Sam Hoatson ran race nights to fundraise for all different kind of things and I often did a night for him. On every race night the sealed films are the same, they are used, resealed and used again, so the operator knows every result. You would think it was a licence to print money but not so. If an operator was to place even a fiver it would totally ruin the odds and would be obvious because the tickets are only 50p and most people only back £1 or £2. Invariably people would come up to me and ask what was going to win and my answer was always the same – 'I will be most surprised if it isn't a horse!' I did a race night for the SNP one night and every one of the organising committee at some point or other asked me for the winner. Bent politicians? Never! What really staggers me is when I think back years to when I took the kids to Butlins. Every day before dinner they had filmed racing in the Gaiety Theatre and since nothing was being raised for charity all the tote cash went into the pay-out pool. The theatre was always full so it would be easy to slip a £5 bet on every race. The Red Coats would have known every winner so they must have cleaned up over the season.

Bobby Elliott had left Mark for a spell to train himself in America; his brother was already an established trainer there but it didn't work out and he came back to Mark after a year or so. A year later he was off again to train on his own at Southport and I often went to stay with him, taking Jock the collie with me. While staying with Bobby I went to the nearby Waterloo Cup at Altcar, greyhound coursing. Every year the animal rights protestors would be there with their placards, trying to disrupt the meeting. They actually got their priorities wrong. The hare would be driven up an open field, the two greyhounds would be hand slipped and the course was on. The animal rights grouse was cruelty to the hare but believe me it was more cruel to the dogs. Most times the hare would escape into the gorse, brambles and rough ground at the top of the field. Greyhound pads are not meant for ground like that so imagine the damage done to their pads and toes. I certainly would never have coursed any of our dogs. My two collies, Nell from my boyhood days or Jock, both raised a hare and caught it at some point while galloping in a field, so it doesn't say a lot for the dogs that couldn't do it. Anyway hunting was eventually banned so the protestors won the war.

Going back again to Jack's training days, a highlight every year was his open day which always attracted thousands and had a massive bar, burger stalls, souvenir stalls etc. Elaine and I took a stall selling our sublimation t-shirts, polo shirts and sweatshirt lines. My daughter Eileen, husband Stevie, in-laws Eddie and Liz, Jock and Jean McDonald, Sam and Rita Hoatson plus friends and family all came down at some time or another, and between staying in Blackpool and going to the open day it was like a mini holiday. My times at Blackpool and Cockerham were becoming more and more frequent and one time Elaine and I passed a car showroom. The cars looked pretty decent and as we were due new cars we stopped to have a look. The owner was called Karl Smith and he and his wife Wendy, as well as son Jeremy and son-in-law Darren, were to become close friends, and from that day on we have always bought our cars from Karl. He is a fanatical Manchester United fan and he often came to Old Trafford with me and was in his element when he met Alex. They also never miss the annual Haydock trip. I take the mickey out of Karl's showroom but believe me I never got a bad deal.

Even further back to before I even met Elaine I had taken my daughters to a caravan park outside Blackpool. We were on the promenade when I bumped into John O'Donnell, the owner of Mount Vernon greyhound track in Glasgow, where Bill and I often ran our dogs. He had three entries in the derby heats that night, Ford (where he lived), Co-op and Society. Each one won, breaking the track record each time, and for good measure three of his Irish pals had runners that also won so what a night we had. The derby was worth £5,000 to the winner, even more than the actual greyhound derby at that time. Two of John's dogs were to reach the final but lost out to a Powderhall-trained dog. For a change of scenery I decided to take the kids over the Whitley Bay for the second week of our holiday. Before we left Blackpool I left a good bet on Jack Nicklaus to win the Open at Turnberry. He looked home and hosed until Tom Watson produced that miracle shot at the 17th in a match that was dubbed The Duel in The Sun.

My daughter gave birth to two daughters, Hayley and Caitlin, and life sailed along at a leisurely pace. When my granddaughters were old enough we all went to Blackpool for Hogmanay – Elaine, me, Eileen and Stevie, Eddie and Liz and the granddaughters. Of all the hundreds of times I've been in Blackpool that was the only bad time. New Year in Blackpool. Never again.

Anyway, back to the present and another pal appeared on the scene, Hank Duncan, and he joined the Old Trafford brigade. He was a real racing man so we got on from day one. I don't see so much of him nowadays as he lives in Thailand and only comes home three or four times a year. Jim Innes is the same, he sold his pubs and hotels and retired to Gran Canaria. Jock McDonald, Eddie Cairns and myself were to go to two successive European Cup Finals in Paris and Milan and we were to meet more celebrities on these trips. The Paris trip was something. Jock and I were both Hearts fans, Eddie a Hibs fan and in one of the bars before the game the ex-Hibs player John Collins and some of the present-day Hibs players were congregating, and as Eddie knew some of them he was in his element. It might sound ignorant but Jock and I chose to drink on our own and left Eddie to it. On the day of the final we had a few beers on the Champs Elysees and meandered up to the Arc de Triomphe, which we ascended, and what a view of Paris we got. However, before we got up the Arc we stood for ages trying to get a gap in the traffic on the huge roundabout surrounding it. We noticed a gendarme watching us then he was joined by another and they appeared to be wetting themselves laughing. Eventually they must have taken pity on us and said, 'M'siuer, underpass' pointing to some stairs. All the time we stood there, there were underground tunnels to the bloody thing. Eejits we felt, eejits we were.

The next year in Milan was something. Every club amateur, professional even the Army is allowed to apply for tickets for a European Final. In those days club directors didn't bother (it's different now tickets are like gold dust) but Jim Innes owned Dumbarton and applied for tickets and we got his allocation of six. A hotel owner I knew in Blackpool owned Walsall so we got six from him too. Our idea was to use three for ourselves and sell the rest to help offset our expenses. However in a chat with Alex Ferguson I had mentioned we were going to the game and to cut a long story short Alex was short of tickets and we had extra so he took them for his assistant Jim Ryan. When we got our tickets we were told we had to have the passport numbers of everyone getting tickets. I didn't have Jim's passport number so I phoned Lyn Laffin for it but Jim had left for the day and Alex was already in Milan as a UEFA guest. After much toing and froing we got it sorted and Jim was to meet us at our hotel and we would go over to the UEFA hotel later that night to give Alex the surplus tickets. To pass the time we went for a walk around and bumped into some of the Bayern Munich players (they were playing Valencia in the final), and being assistant manager of Manchester United Jim was recognised immediately, a conversation struck up and it was a great experience to meet the German superstars. We went to the UEFA hotel that night and what a place. Italian hotels are luxurious on the whole but this was something else. The first person we saw was Mick Hucknall from Simply Red – another staunch United fan – he gave Alex a shout and the tickets were handed over. Alex, courteous as he always is, blethered to us for a minute or two and as Hibs were playing Celtic in the Scottish Cup Final that weekend Eddie asked him what he thought. He was right miffed when informed that Alex thought Celtic would easily rattle five in, which in fact they did. It just wasn't Eddie's night. We left the hotel to get a taxi into the Plaza in the city centre and while we were waiting outside a club a couple of scantily clad women sauntered up to Eddie saying, 'You come to our club, yes?' Something didn't ring true and a local Italian, also in the taxi queue, fortunately spoke good English and said to me, 'My friend, does your friend there know that is a transvestite club?' Eddie never lived that one down. We eventually got to the Plaza and Eddie got the first round in, three small beers, £27. We drank up smartly and were just leaving when the owner of one of our locals back home, Ally McCoist and a few others were on their way in. We tipped them the wink about the prices so we all set off together and eventually found a bar, which though dear was reasonable. As I said, it just wasn't Eddie's night.

The final the following year was at Hampden and Alex being a Govan man was desperate for United to win it on his home patch. It wasn't to be; Real Madrid rather luckily beat them and went on to win it. However, as he was sure they would do it he wanted as many tickets as he could get for friends and family. Gordon McDougall who Jim Innes had known for years owned

Cowdenbeath and was on the SFA committee. The SFA erected a large marquee in Lesser Hampden where you could book a table for a pre-match meal and entertainment and the package included a match ticket. I told Alex and he took advantage of the deal, and though he didn't use them he wasn't left out of pocket as he managed to dispose of them. Another twist to the story is the time Davy and I were at the Marriot Hotel in London and Steve Archibald was at our table. The conversation came up about the SFA package and Archibald being an ex-Spanish League player wanted tickets for his Spanish lawyer. When I told him Alex had tickets he asked for his number so he could ring him and see if he had any spare. No way, I said, I will give you the office number, call Lyn and talk to her. I never liked Archibald as a player and meeting him in person I liked him even less. He said, 'I've known Alex longer than you, I played for him at Aberdeen.' I replied, 'I couldn't give a you know what if you played for him at pocket billiards, you are not getting his number.' When I told Alex he said, 'well done, the only way he would get tickets from me would be cash up front and only after making sure the notes were kosher.'

By now our annual trips to Haydock and Old Trafford had swelled to over 40, not always all at once but enough so that Karl Smith had dubbed us Alan's Army. There were a few bad apples now and then but they were soon found out and elbowed, but in general terms a better bunch of lads you couldn't meet. Somewhere or other I've mentioned them all except Charlie Boyd and his brother Kevin, whose assistance in the admin side of things has been an immense help to me and David Currie, who has been a regular almost from day one.

Jock the collie and I continued about our merry way, going about our business at the resort hotels and what a pal he was. The miles we covered over hill and dale and his favourite beaches kept me as fit as I had ever been. The hotel business had steadied as the signs I made lasted for life, but I was still supplying sheets, towels and I was having a purple patch with the jewellery I bought from Clive. Good as things were, nothing is forever, especially life itself. When I started this book I mentioned all the wonderful relatives I had but father time doesn't stand still and one by one over the next six or seven years I was to say goodbye to them all. Everyone was a heartbreak but losing my mother was unbelievable. We didn't always see eye to eye, mainly because of my gambling which she detested, but I loved her dearly and she loved me too, and it's when that last moment comes and she is gone you realise just what you have lost.

I had 12 of the happiest years of my life with my collie Jock. We were inseparable every night, he would lie at the foot of my bed and every morning there he was waiting for his walk. From Aberdeen to Bridlington on the east coast and Ayr to Southport on the west, he went everywhere with me. He went to every racecourse I went to and although my pals I daresay didn't like the idea of sharing a room with a dog it was that or cramp up in the car because I insisted Jock was comfortable, so they didn't dare say anything. Then one day at 12 years old he was drinking to excess and diabetes was diagnosed. This condition led to blindness, he couldn't run on the beaches and parks any more but brilliant, natural dog that he was he didn't let his condition bother him as long as I was with him. He was fine for the next two years but then developed a lump on his stomach which was diagnosed as cancerous. An operation could possibly have cured it but at 14 years old I wasn't prepared to put him through that. Then one night he coughed all night, I sat up with him but in the morning when he didn't eat his breakfast for the first time in his life and didn't want to walk I had no option but to call the vet and after discussing things had to make the hardest decision of my life. I still miss him terribly and if the truth be told I've never got over losing him. Digging his grave would have been unbearable but John McDonald, Jock's son, who always refers to me as his uncle, came along and did it for me. Elaine and I will be eternally grateful to him. Jock is buried beside Ben and I tend their graves faithfully, from January to March they are covered in snowdrops, daffodils, crocuses and tulips and through the summer a glorious array of summer flowers.

CHAPTER SIX

I have read every one of Alex Ferguson's books and if you haven't I suggest you do as well. There is not one line, verse or chapter that doesn't make sense, they are honest, factual and educational. There was never a thing I've disagreed with in reading from his books or speaking to him personally, until one chapter in his latest book on the comparisons of players through each decade up to the present. He and hundreds of others are 90 per cent right but I would beg to differ on some points. Present-day players Cristiano Ronaldo and Lionel Messi are true world-class, although the German captain Philip Lahm isn't far behind and Luis Suarez and Sergio Aguero are out and out brilliant. There are a raft of other stars but let's do the comparisons. Take Manchester United today against the Busby Babes or the 1968 European Cup-winning squad. Not a single United player today would make these two squads, but anyone of these two squads would make today's team. From the 50s on, take the great names and you will find they would be great whatever generation they played in. Stanley Matthews, Tom Finney, Billy Wright, Dave Mackay, George Young, Willie Waddell, Duncan Edwards and virtually all his teammates, Gordon Smith, Ferenc Puskas, Alfredo di Stefano, Pele, Gento, Santa Maria, the 1966 England World Cup-winning squad, Beckenbauer, Denis Law, George Best, Gary Lineker and so on up to the present, then work back. Take the older players

– Alex ran two pubs to supplement his income, Willie Bauld was a newsagent, as was Johnny Hamilton, Gordon Smith, Lawrie Reilly, Willie Ormond and Jimmy Millar all also ran pubs. Even further back players especially in Northumberland would do a shift down the pit then play for their club. Imagine any of today's lot doing that. I know times have changed and modern players have sponsors, own property, etc, but pound-for-pound in ability give me the old timers any day. Money nowadays of course is different. When Dave Mackay left Hearts of the start of the 60s he was on £20 a week, which rose considerably when he joined Spurs. Alex was on £2,000 a year when he joined Aberdeen and £25,000 when he left and was originally offered even less from Manchester United. He is a multi-millionaire now and has earned every penny. True, in the old days when Davy got £20 a week your man in the street was on £4 or £5 (my first wage was two pounds and ten shillings) so your footballers were well paid. Fitness wise nowadays with all the modern equipment and medical teams etc they should be fitter but I don't think they are. That's the big teams but look at the wider picture, your lower divisions, juniors and amateurs. They are no fitter now, most probably less so than 50 years ago. Fifty years ago kids had nothing to do but play day and night. Nowadays there are so many distractions and with the junk food available their diet certainly won't be better, so give me the older generations every time.

In other sports its true as well that the present generation is different. In motor racing, take Stirling Moss and Mike Hawthorn versus Lewis Hamilton and Michael Schumacher and of course the former couldn't compete in their old antique cars, but if time travel were possible then the results would be the same. In athletics, the present crop are fitter and faster and have more time to train, with better tracks and equipment, but they also have drugs. In my younger days the only dope we knew was the village idiot. Athletics would probably be the exception as every year a fraction of a second will be shaved off a world record but that fraction doesn't put them poles apart. Boxing? No contest, the old brigade are streets ahead, Rocky Marciano, Cassius Clay, George Foreman, Sonny Liston, Joe Frazier would totally destroy anyone from Mike Tyson to Tyson Fury. It must be said of the present crop, Tyson Fury will beat Wilder to regain his world title and will beat Joshua. Billy Jo Saunders is a world champion at two weights and that is top class in any era. Tennis is the same, Andy Murray, Djokovic, Federer and Nadal against Borg, Connors and Sampras? There's nothing in it. Golf as well, when I was stationed in Troon in 1963 in the Army and the Open was played there, Arnold Palmer shot a 68 on the last day. The par at Troon is still 72, the courses are better and easier now but the scores are still the same so that makes the old brigade look better.

Back to football though. In the 50s and 60s they played with a heavy T ball, which was soaked in dubbin on a wet day and weighed a ton. The boots were like miner's safety boots with leather studs if not nailed in right played havoc with your feet. The jerseys were heavy duty cotton, especially the goalkeepers, which also weighed a ton in the wet. Today's lot could never handle that gear, but Dave Mackay could blast that T ball in from 30 yards out. Then you have today's managers sitting with a clipboard writing notes, Manchester United's last manager Louis Van Gaal had a big red book and I thought he was going to do an Eammon Andrews and say at half time, 'Sir Alex Ferguson, this is your life'. It never happened in the old days. Then there is Scottish football, which is a joke. Two Englishmen run it, Stuart Reagan at the SFA and Neil Doncaster at the SPFL, and though they have committees they are the mouthpieces. You also have what every Scottish fan knows as the gravy train, and once you are on that you never want off it. They have taken Scottish football to an all-time low and some of the old timers would turn in their graves if they saw the present situation. At one time the English league teemed with brilliant Scottish players but not now. The Scottish league doesn't even have one. It's a crying shame when you see the work that people like Jim Stevenson and Anne Budge do for their clubs and the efforts Dave King and his consortium are making to restore Rangers.

So, anyway, Elaine and I were now celebrating 30 years together and it was again held in Blackpool and Haydock, with two of the greatest friends I have now about to appear on the scene, Willie Wightman and his wife Corrine. Willie is another great guy and a true gentleman.

A few years ago Sam Hoatson and I went to Old Trafford for a Wedneseday night game and in Alex's suite afterward we briefly met the Coolmore Mob, JP McManus and John Magnier. We only spoke briefly, hello, pleased to meet you, best of luck at York with your horses. Sam and I travelled to

Scarborough the next day and commuted to York every day for the Dante race meeting. We were coming out of the course after the last race when we passed McManus. I said hello and he looked at me like I was shit on his shoe. I told Alex not to trust them an inch, as did Jim Innes, but he reckoned Magnier was a gentleman. How right we were proved, they were only after Manchester United for the quick profit which was what they achieved, but in doing so they played dirty with Alex. Need I add Jock the collie was still with us at that time and came to York and we had a good week covering our expenses and spending the last night with Bobby Elliott at Leyburn.

Well, you may have noticed, gambling is a subject which has frequently cropped up in this book, so what can I tell you about what I've learned? I have told you about some nice touches I've had in my time but now let me tell you about the evils of it. As most of my friends will tell you I could and should have been a millionaire two or three times over. Hard work was never a problem and I always had the ability to earn a healthy shilling. Gambling didn't ruin my marriage but it could have and I am lucky to still have Elaine after she has seen what I have squandered over the years. Sure I was always lucky with my dogs and when Jack Berry was training I won more than I lost and I have always been lucky at cards. Horses have always been my downfall. My first piece of advice is to stay clear of odds-on favourites and watch closely the jockeys and trainers that are allergic to them. One jockey in that category is one of the top ten and he has been beaten on seven odds-on favourites in the last two weeks as I write this. Try and be selective. You can't back six winners every day. In my entire life I have been through the card only three times and they were all short priced. The game nowadays is more unpredictable than it ever was. Stand in any pub or betting shop any day of the week and watch some of the blatant cheating, 100 people will see it, comment on it and no way can they all be wrong. You need strong stewards to control it, and they do but they are in a minority. I know it is hard to prove a jockey is actually cheating even when he blatantly is, all he has to say is the horse didn't find when I asked it. The At The Races team are good, their phone and email lines are constantly revealing viewers' gripes and views on blatant cheating and they air them. As I said, be as selective as you can, concentrate on the big meetings and try and follow trainers and jockeys who are in form. In four or five horse races where the favourite is long odds on and the second favourite is nailed on for the forecast, don't touch it. Seven times out of 10 the second favourite doesn't try a leg and nothing is ever said. One trainer to follow is Willie Mullins, sure a lot of his horses, in fact most, are odds-on but a winner is a winner. If Willie does have a horse beaten you can be sure you will recoup your losses. His success is helped by the fact he has the greatest jump jockey of all time Ruby Walsh to boot his winners home and his son PW Mullins is nearly impossible to beat in bumpers. Nina Carberry usually wins what PW doesn't and is another jockey to follow, she wouldn't know how to cheat. Simon Walker in amateur riders' races is another who is almost unbeatable. A recent incident where the punter has no chance was the last race at a meeting when the jockey Aidan Coleman was beaten on a 4-9 chance. Not a single punter thought anything other than it didn't try a leg and Coleman was attacked by a couple of punters after the race. I must say he is one of the best and straightest jockeys around and I am not condoning it, especially as it wasn't a one-on-one confrontation, but look at the wider picture. The stewards and the papers crucified the culprits but I never heard anyone ask why they had done it. Obviously it was because they felt they had been cheated. I can recall similar incidents in the past. Beaten favourites are often booed on returning to the enclosure. Tony McCoy had a full beer can thrown at him. On a Scottish Grand National Day the trainer Jenny Pitman slapped the face of her jockey Jamie Osbourne in public for his riding of her horse. Jo Berry used to say a lot of punters talk out of their pocket and I am sure that's true on the facts I've mentioned, but at the same time there is no smoke without fire. When I have stayed with Bobby Elliott in Leyburn three jockeys have at different times told me they were on the fiddle. I won't name them as it would be my word against theirs and they could sue, but I assure you it's true. Musselburgh, my home course is a good course for winning favourites, the stewards are vigilant, and all in all you get a good honest run for your money. There are always exceptions but I can honestly say Musselburgh is one course where I have won more than I have lost. Haydock is another course where I have had a good percentage in favour of fancied horses.

The lady trainers Venetia Williams, Rebecca Curtis and Lucinda Russell are never far away, as is Diane Sayer, you always get a fair run from them. Peter Bowen and his son are a trainer jockey combination who you also always get value for money with, as are the Skelton brothers Dan and Harry. John Ferguson does well with the hurdlers he recruits from the flat. One trainer to keep a keen eye is Keith Dalglish, he will go right to the top. I know Keith well; in fact, Jock the collie and I once stayed at his house. It's only my opinion but of all the jockeys Mark Johnston has used Keith is right at the top. Like Bobby Elliott, he was champion apprentice and had increasing weight not caused his premature retirement he could well have been champion jockey. As a trainer he has made a great start and his horses can be followed with confidence. Another good trainer to follow is Kevin Ryan who I know from his days as head lad to Jack Berry. He too is hitting the heights as a trainer and just shows Jack didn't only produce winning horses. Two knowledgeable people to listen to are Gordon Brown who co-hosts the Racing Channel. I've known Gordon for years and he actually did a great job on the top table at one of the dinners we had for Jack. He reads a race well, is as honest as they come, and if he tips a horse it won't be far way. Compared to presenters like McCririck and McGrath, he is in a league of his own. The second person is the former UK Racing presenter Ifty Ahmed. There isn't much Ifty doesn't know about racing and anything he tells you listen to. Ifty and his son Naz were to become great friends when we were all regulars at Blackpool. There aren't many sporting events Ifty isn't clued up on and he is fanatical about Manchester United, following them home and way. He was actually at Alex Ferguson's first and last matches as manager. It is also wise to remember trainers don't train for the public but for their owners, so don't always listen to tips given as connections want the best price and don't want their horses' chances bandied about.

Away from racing, but still along the gambling theme, another good piece of advice is to never, ever play one-armed bandits; you may put in £1 and drop the jackpot but how often in your life will that happen? The machines even tell you they pay out 76 per cent, they don't care who wins the jackpot they are guaranteed £24 in every £100. Casinos are another no no. I often go to our local casino for a meal but I don't bet. I did get told a system that works but it's like watching paint dry. You pick a colour red or black and a number odd or even and put your fiver or whatever on each. Time after time you only cover your bet but when the two come up you win. As I said I don't bet in casinos but I did give Elaine money once to try the system. She chose red even and after almost three hours she amassed £110 from her original tenner, so it works, but as I said, paint drying. I can hold my own on football bets. Two bets I like are first goalscorer and no goal. No goal usually pays about 9-1 and if the first goal is an own goal you still win on anything after that. When a team is going well more often than not the first goalscorer is its main striker. Ronaldo and Messi are regular first scorers. Another good bet when you are watching a live game is to take a draw half time and full time. It pays good odds so if you get your draw at half time you can bet in running on the second half and manipulate things to suit you – i.e. if it's still a draw with 10 minutes to go and looks like staying that way you can back both teams to win and you can't lose. That's what I should have done at Dens Park all those years ago but that's a painful memory. Avoid Russian and Turkish teams playing at home and avoid the African Nations games as they are too unpredictable. So there you have 50 years of advice, please don't make the same mistakes I did.

CHAPTER SEVEN

A s we near the end of this story and before it reaches its amazing climax, I will drift back to any worthwhile stories I have missed. There were two in the toy trade. I was at Harrogate and placed an order for reams of Christmas wrapping paper. I reckoned I needed about 5,000 sheets and told the rep to convert that into 100-odd reams. He misunderstood and sent me 5,000 reams, enough to keep Lapland going forever. The company agreed to pick them up but never did. I know that sounds ludicrous but it's the honest truth. I phoned time after time and even saw them every year at Harrogate for the next few years and still they never showed. Totally amazing. The second occurrence was securing the biggest order I ever had. In every town or city you have a shopping mall or precinct. My local one in Edinburgh was part of a chain also covering Livingston, Glasgow, Belfast, Manchester, Liverpool and Leeds, which was their head office. The manager of the Edinburgh mall became friendly with me when we met at the dogs. He wasn't a big gambler but he and his wife liked their night at the track and I gave them a few winners. He placed the order for his mall with me but said the chief executive would be in Edinburgh the next week and he would arrange a meeting with him to discuss the possibility of me supplying all the centres. As luck would have it the chief executive and his wife were real greyhound regulars at

Elland Road in Leeds and liked it so much they were thinking about buying a greyhound themselves, and asked my advice. I knew a Leeds trainer and got them a really good dog at a good price. The result was I got the entire order, and what an order – 25,000 wrapped toys! Now here is where near miracles were worked. Every kid who visited Santa's Grotto got a present but the budget was £1.75 per head and what can you really get for that? This was November and the toys had to be wrapped and delivered by 1 December. Firstly with the size of the order and some wheeling and dealing with my suppliers I got a range to suit the chief executive at his price with a good profit for Elaine and me. The girls worked day and night to wrap them and everything was ready on time. The arrangement was I would deliver to Edinburgh, Livingston, Glasgow and Belfast before going on to Leeds, where they would deliver to Manchester and Liverpool themselves. I hired a lorry and did the Belfast and Leeds drops in three days. Everything worked like clockwork and the chief executive was so impressed that we did it on schedule that he actually paid me for the lot on arrival at his head office. As I said, for £1.75 you don't get a lot but we managed and one of the lines was a plastic potato gun. Within days I had a frantic call from the Belfast shopping mall manager screaming about me supplying guns. Now let's face it, troubles or not, I hardly think even the most trigger-happy soldier is going to mistake a kid with a potato gun for a terrorist. Does it also mean that Irish kids can't play Cowboys and Indians? Do you withhold knitting sets from the girls because the needles could be offensive weapons or battery operated toys because the batteries could be used as detonators? We sorted it out and Belfast sent the toy guns to Leeds and we sent replacement toys to Belfast and everybody was happy. That order lasted three years and only ended because the precinct Santas stopped giving toys out. The reason? Women being women, there were continual moans about the toys being paltry. The chief executive was at pains to point out to me it wasn't our fault, that he was delighted with our service and quality of goods but their budget was £1.75 and you only get what you pay for so the toys had to be stopped. I don't know who was most disappointed, the toy wrappers or me. They still wrapped the club toys and made good money but 25,000 toys at 10p each was a real blow to them.

The other story appertaining to the toy trade at Harrogate was a night Elaine and I were in our favourite restaurant in the Western Saloon. The entire place was decorated like an old wild-west saloon and the menu was fantastic. They had a special offer with a 16oz T-bone steak or a 2lb beefburger and if you ate either in a certain time your meal was free. A crowd of reps came in and took the table next to us. One of them was about 5ft 6in and I have seen more fat on a chip than he carried but he devoured the steak in half the allotted time and when one of the crowd couldn't finish his burger he devoured that as well. I was speaking to one of the reps later and remarked on the wee fella, the bloke told me, 'That's nothing, he wasn't particularly hungry tonight'. I said I would hate to share a room with him and the bloke replied that nobody in the company would share a room with him! Another famous for his flatulence is a lifelong friend who I won't name. Now this friend can't pass a McDonald's and he can eat for Scotland but he is also a world-class farter. On our trips his son is forced to room share with him and it's so bad the cleaners have to put a canary in the room before they service it. I would have loved to have pitted my pal against the lad at Harrogate then put them in the same room. They would have activated every alarm in the hotel.

Another incident worth mentioning is one that shows how pompous and aloof course executives and stewards can be. Many years ago when Jack Berry was at the absolute peak of his career he had his Red Shirt night at Pontefract to fundraise for his injured jockeys fund. Two of his owners, his top two in fact, Chris and Antonia Deutens, an absolutely marvellous couple, sponsored one of the races. The winning owner could have a trophy or cash to the value of the trophy, or that was what Pontefract said. I had never heard of this before, you usually got your prize money and a trophy. With my fancy goods I had a really attractive range of Killarney Crystal and Chris and Antonia asked me to supply them with a beautiful decanter and six glasses set on a silver tray. I arranged with my suppliers to send it direct to Pontefract, which they did, packed in a way which was totally unbreakable. The race was run and a week later I got a call from the chief executive, a pompous arrogant man, saying the winning owner had taken cash instead of the crystal and he was sending it back. It came back OK, in a million pieces. The clown hadn't even packed it in any way just stuck it in a box. When I raised the matter with Gundell he simply said claim on your insurance. How arrogant and stupid can you get? They dispatched the parcel so it was their place to claim from the firm they used. Anyway, I wrote the loss off but I've never been back and never will be back to Pontefract.

Moving on, as I told you earlier, Elaine was the female vocal in the group at the Palais nightclub in Edinburgh in her younger days. I had met the singer Marty Wilde when he appeared in the PO's Mess at Rosyth and one time when we were at the NEC in Birmingham he was there promoting a new line called a karaoke machine. He recognised me and we got to blethering and he told me, 'Alan, trust me, this is going to be the next craze to sweep the nation.' The stand was mobbed and Marty and Elaine sang a duet to rapturous applause. Elaine said, 'Buy it, it's a sure-fire winner'. Daft arse here said, 'Elaine, who in their right mind is going to stand in a boozer and sing to a TV screen?' I never lived that one down. Talking about the PO's Mess at Rosyth, they didn't half get some acts. Money was no object so they went for the best. I met the Alexander Brothers and in fact shared a room one night with Tom. Jack went home after their act but Tom stayed on to socialise. We got blethering and pissed as newts, far too drunk to drive, so the Navy gave us bed and breakfast for the night. Others I met and became friendly with were Hector Nicol, Alex 'Happy' Howden, Phil Clark Jr, and Sydney Devine. Some of them actually bought my digital watches and leather gear. Eat your heart out Del Boy.

I will go back to a breathtaking incident that happened to me in the 50s when the King George whisky distillery caught fire. As the crow flies our house Catherine Bank was only 800 yards away and our view was spectacular. The exploding vats shot flames high into the night sky and the whole town was illuminated. Every house in the vicinity was evacuated and at one point we thought we were going to have to leave our home. It was reminiscent of the old film Whisky Galore where the villagers collected kegs of whisky washed ashore from a wrecked ship and customs and police just couldn't cope with the hordes who plundered the beach. This time though it was Shangri la for the locals. The distillery was situated half way up a steep hill called the Loan and the whisky from the exploding vats ran down the hill into the main street like a river in full spate. The locals were out all night with basins, buckets, tin baths, anything that could contain liquid. If there was anything the police could do about it they didn't, they were probably working the scam themselves. It took about three days to fully extinguish the fire.

During my greyhound days there was one New Year's Day that would be one I would never forget. Bobby Christie, my racing partner at that time, fed and washed the dogs in the morning and I was to do the evening kennels after the Hearts Hibs game at Tynecastle. I knew it was a bad day when Hearts lost 7-0 but what was to follow was like a scene from Texas Chainsaw Massacre. I got to the kennels and wondered why it was so quiet. I was soon to find out. Bobby, the old fool, had forgotten to muzzle the dogs and they had fought and torn chunks out of each other. It looked bad with blood everywhere but I separated them, muzzled them then started to check the damage. Miraculously no veins had been damaged or tendons torn. I then immediately phoned Roger Baird the vet at Powderhall who lived 25 miles away in Haddington and he said to bring them into the surgery. Our van could hold five at a push but not the 10 that were injured so Roger said, 'I'm on my, do what you can until I get there'. Roger arrived at about 8 o'clock and we worked six hours solid until 2am, me boiling water, cleaning instruments and applying ointment and bandages as instructed, Roger doing the stitching and any other major work. Some people, probably because he was a country vet, thought Roger a bit rough but not in a million years, his work that night was the best veterinary work I have ever seen. It wasn't worthwhile going to bed as I had to be up early again to check the dogs and as I lived nearby we went back to my house to clean up. Roger had a bottle in the car and I had some beers and spirits in the house so we tore in for our belated New Year drink. As the conversation went on and I mentioned as a boy it had been my ambition to be a vet, Roger said, 'Believe me, what I have seen in the last few hours there is no way you wouldn't have been a good vet'. I never pursued my ambition and that's history now, but it was nice to know a true professional thought I could have done it. Operations, the gore and the muck would never have bothered me, but I don't know if I would have been up for seeing people bring their terminally ill pet in, put it to sleep, then watch them break their hearts.

We are now well established with our Blackpool and Haydock trips, and you've heard about a number of them, everybody knows everybody like the back of their hands and a better bunch you could not find. Just to put the record straight, let me tell you just how highly I respect and admire them.

Every man and woman I have mentioned in my story would have made a better Prime Minister than any we have had since the war. Rubbish you say? I think not. With what they have achieved, either by reaching the top in sport or in forming and developing their own company, at least 12 of them would automatically fill the PM's position and without doubt do it as it should be done. If not filling the PM's role they would form a powerful cabinet and the ladies come into the same category as the men. Elaine, Anne Stevenson, Wendy Smith, my cousin Penelope and Erica Hill would all, without even breaking sweat, supersede anything any woman politician has accomplished, perhaps excepting Thatcher. You doubt my sanity in making such statements? Let's analyse it then. The requirements for the post of Prime Minister, cabinet minister or MP are above-average intelligence, the ability to work hard with or without supervision, honesty and willingness to travel. The riff raff we've had since the war? Intelligence pass marks for some, but hard work and honesty? Enter the names I would nominate and it wouldn't be a contest.

If you want further clarification let me tell you three stories about a soldier turned politician who would be included in my group and two politicians not worth a balloon and birler. The first story concerns Tam Dalyell, who was MP for my boyhood area and an out and out pacifist, any talk of military action and he was always the first to object. In fact rumour has it if you farted loudly near to Dalyell he would dive for the nearest air raid shelter. What he and a certain General Philip Towers did to a superb soldier and his equally superb regiment was a cowardly disgrace. The Argyll and Sutherland Highlanders were due to replace the Northumberland Fusiliers in Aden and they were commanded by Lt Col Colin Mitchell. The outgoing rear party of the Fusiliers were showing the Argylls the layout of a real dump called Crater Town when they were ambushed. They were tortured and burned and left where they fell. General Towers was a play it safe merchant and ordered the recapture of Crater Town but in two stages over two nights. His plan was the Argylls would attack from one side and the Commandos the other, they would meet in the middle, secure their positions and mop up the next day. Stupidity, forewarned is forearmed and Mitchell had no intention of giving them any warning or showing any mercy. He attacked with a vengeance, sweeping through the entire area and securing the whole shooting match in a matter of hours. The Commandos probably had the same idea (these units don't know the meaning of the phrase go easy) but Mitchell beat them to the punch. The outcome was Towers, rat that he was, while managing to claim credit for a successful action threatened action against Mitchell for disobeying orders. Dalyell was all over the papers also slamming Mitchell and his regiment as irresponsible, negligent and any other words he had just learned to spell. Mitchell would have progressed to become a general but Towers effectively put a huge dent in his career. Later in life I would pick Mitchell up at Waverly Station and take him to meet my boss General Lusk.

Another time many years later Elaine and I were having a meal at our favourite sea food restaurant in Blackpool when the MP for our constituency in Edinburgh came in, who I won't name. The party conference was on and a party of ten or so came in and sat at the next table to us. I watched them order and they bought the dearest starter, main course and dessert, drank the dearest wine and brandy. The main man paid the whole bill and then each individual asked for a separate itemised bill. Work that one out for yourselves. Let's say that happened all over town that night, how much do you reckon it cost the taxpayer? Blackpool certainly sees it all. Apart from what goes on in the conferences their councillors closely followed by my home city of Edinburgh bear more scrutiny than most. When we were at our peak with the sublimation sign printing I was approached by a councillor who ran his own business supplying hotels with personalised calendars and cards. He was interested in the safety signs I produced for the hotels. It cost me £4 to make one and I sold it for £6. This guy covered the country and I arranged to post his orders at £5 a sign plus postage, warning him that Blackpool was mine. About a year later when I began in Scarborough the first hotel Jock and I stayed at had my signs behind the door. When I mentioned it to the owner she confirmed it was indeed the councillor who supplied them at £14 a sign. How's that for daylight robbery, and he wasn't the worst of the Blackpool brigade. Edinburgh got rid of our trams 60 years ago but some bright spark on the council decided to reinstate them. It ran hundreds of millions over budget, was way over time on completion and only covered half the original intended route. It caused utter chaos in the city, they tore up the town and the half that wasn't completed had to be re-laid at more cost. This caused near financial ruin to the shops in the area as people couldn't get access. Not one single Edinburgh citizen wanted the trams but the council went ahead and you don't have to be Einstein to figure how many pockets bulged as a result.

Back now to January 2013 and the sad news that Dave Mackay, who hasn't been in the best of health recently, is deteriorating. Alex Ferguson, who thought the world of Dave, as did Dave of him, and myself organised one last tribute to Dave. It was to be held in the Premier Inn at Old Trafford on 4 July. It was an appropriate venue as we were always welcomed there and had tables reserved by Vince Ward on our weekend visits and Dave was always bombarded by well-wishers and autograph hunters. He happily accommodated every request made of him. It took a full six months organising and I took care of all admin arrangements while Alex organised the top table, and what a table it was. All Davy's family from Derby and Edinburgh were in attendance, as were all the crowd who had congregated every year for the past 18 years. We all stayed at the Park House Hotel in Blackpool for the weekend. The proceedings started with a night at Haydock races on the Friday night. It was a superb night and just about everybody won as we had received some good tips. Everyone had a relaxing Saturday before leaving for the dinner. Alex did Davy proud with the top table, which consisted of Alex, Davy and Isobel, Davy's trusty assistant manager Des Anderson and his wife Lesley, Denis Law, Martin Buchan, Pat Crerand, Dandy Nicholls, Billy Hunter, Lorraine Summers, one of Scotland's top comedians who did the after-dinner cabaret, and her partner Kenny Paton and I compered the night. It was a fantastic success and was to be Davy's last real public appearance and he loved it. We recorded the night on DVD and it is a real collectors' item.

When I look back on that night and watch the DVD it makes me feel privileged to think just how much we have shared and how much they have all come to mean to me. Who would have thought that Jock Macdonald and I who were once boys together in Queensferry would one day be leading the tributes to our boyhood idol? The crowd was immense and before the event I had all the top table in a private room to give them a bit of privacy. I was sitting beside Martin Buchan and Pat Crerand and mentioned that along with Davy they were the best players I had ever seen. I even compared them to Beckenbauer, and Martin asked me what planet I was on. I reasoned that if they had been German they would probably have played for Bayern and certainly Germany. Beckenbauer was the same in reverse so all in all there wasn't a lot in it. Alex Ferguson was immense in his efforts to honour Davy. He was due to leave early the next morning for a much earned family holiday but nothing would stop him from honouring a great man. The event started at 7.30 and finished at midnight but it didn't end there. I had brought three coachloads from Blackpool and on our return instead of going into the town we socialised until the small hours at the Park House. Back at the Premier Inn Davy's family, Alan Short's party, the Irish contingent and Martin Buchan and his friends from Aberdeen did the same. There were a few sore heads the next day as we all made our way home but it was a night to remember.

Between starting proceedings in January and the event in July, Alex announced his retirement. What a career he had. No one will ever achieve what he accomplished, 30 trophies in 26 years at Old Trafford not to mention his phenomenal success at Aberdeen before that. I may add that phenomenal success denied Davy and my beloved Hearts the league and cup double. When we went to Old Trafford on our Blackpool weekends Alex always made time to come down and meet us. Every one of us will be eternally grateful.

We had another tribute night the following March again in Blackpool this time for Martin Buchan and Dandy Nicholls. Dandy and his wife Alexis are superb trainers and like Alex he has set records that will never be beaten, six Ayr Gold Cups plus just about every other major sprint in the racing calendar. He is an avid Manchester United fan but a real football man and most knowledgeable in just about any sport you care to name. He is very much like Alex in that he would have been a success no matter what sport he chose. We went to Haydock again in July and had another full house and were joined by another gem of a lady, Joanne Moncur, who ran Dandy's racing club. Dandy also joined us that night purely to enjoy some time off and brought along one of his close pals Mark Furness, who is a jockeys agent, and his partner Angela. They have also become close pals and come to love their time at Blackpool.

The saddest part of the story now comes with the news that Dave Mackay had finally succumbed to his illness which he fought as bravely as he fought in every game in his illustrious career. His funeral was held in Edinburgh and was superbly organised by the love of his life, apart from his family of course, Heart of Midlothian FC. It was impossible to get every one of his pals who enjoyed our weekends away into the official ceremony so I had to be fair in the selection of who would attend from our side. Isobel said obviously Alex and myself and Denis Law, who travelled up with Alex. Alex's brother Martin was a must, as was Martin Buchan, and I added his other good pals from our trips Jock Macdonald, Jim Stevenson and Kenny Paton. Thousands lined the streets, Spurs sent a large delegation including some of Davy's surviving teammates. I met up with Frank McLintock again; we were sat next to each other. All the Hearts players were there as well as a contingent from Derby County and ex-players from all over.

One absentee was the man Dave gave his big break in English football, Rene Meulensteen. I don't know the reason why. He will be sadly missed by us all and his like will never be seen again. The one thing I am glad he didn't do was take the player-manager's job at Tynecastle years earlier. He told me he had seriously considered it but rightly added that it's never the same second time round, and how right he was. Everyone now can remember him as the greatest talent Hearts ever had. One regret he did have was that he never played with or under Alex Ferguson. What a team that would have been. They did play against each other once but it was only a reserve game Hearts v Queens Park. He overcame two badly broken legs and mouth cancer and was still a colossus. Compared to players nowadays if you had mentioned broken metatarsal or hamstring to Davy he would have asked what track they were running at and if they were worth backing. Davy never lost his love for Hearts and like every Hearts fan got sick of hearing our city rivals crow about the 7-0 New Year's Day hiding they gave us. Truth was the game wasn't on the radio, only got the winners two points and neither team won anything that season, and in the next two matches between the teams Hearts rammed home nine goals. Davy was to live to see Hearts completely wipe out the 7-0 embarrassment when they totally annihilated Hibs on two occasions, the first in a cup semi-final where Gretna awaited the winners in the final. The semi was over long before the end, with Hearts romping away and going on to lift the trophy. The next humiliation was in the final itself a couple of years later when Hearts won 5-1. Even then Davy didn't gloat, at least not openly. At his funeral I met the saviour of Hearts when they were down and almost out, Anne Budge. I only spoke to her briefly but told her how proud Davy would have been to know her and she genuinely seemed to appreciate it. She hasn't half put Hearts back on track.

Life goes on and when we had our usual weekend in Blackpool and at Old Trafford just a few weeks ago a cracker of a laugh happened. We had returned from the game and I was in my room getting changed when Ifty Ahmed came to my door saying an ex-West Ham player called Patsy Holland was downstairs in the lounge. He was nothing to me but seemed to impress the lads. He said he was retired and was an executive for Samsung and was in Blackpool to organise accommodation for the company's AGM. He offered the lads cut-price phones and welcomed them to Upton Park where he said he had a box.

Someone mentioned I was friendly with Dave Mackay and Alex Ferguson and the bold boy said I remember Dave – he definitely didn't but next time you see him tell him all his forgiven. He said any time he had met Alex he was hard work. I said not at all and in fact I have his latest book in my room, read it and learn. The book was marked £25 but I bought it in Tesco for £12 and I sold it to him for £20, and I then told the lads (Ifty had already figured it out) that he was a fraud. Everyone in the football world knew Davy had died and Alex was never hard work to anyone unless they gave him cause to be. Ifty had checked him out and found his real name was George Smith and he had done time for impersonating Patsy Holland, who he was the image of. He was convincing though but as I have said you have to be prepared for anything and anyone in Blackpool. Mind you this clown couldn't have sold my mates anything that was a privilege reserved for me. I have told you about this marvellous crowd of people I have managed to bring together over the years and there is one thing they all have in common, they trust me implicitly. I am sure sometimes they were more interested in what I was flogging and when they went home their wives would say, 'What's he flogged you this time?' Usually it was jewellery for them so I never got the rough edge of their tongues. Mind you everything I flogged them was a bargain. The really funny part was the English and Irish lads said I was Scotland's answer to Del Boy. The Scots lads said not in a million years, Del Boy is England's answer to Alan. Even Ifty doesn't try and bargain with me. That's all tongue in cheek but the real truth is that if the lads want anything they will usually ask to get it for them. It works two ways as well and if I have ever been in trouble or needed anything I only had to ask and they were there for me. Million dollar gold nuggets each and every one of them. I may add that anyone reading this can meet some of the characters. We go to the Haydock evening meeting the first Friday in July and anyone turning up will be made welcome.

That brings me to the end of my story and I would like to express my thanks before I close. To my mother who brought me into this world, and made it possible for my daughters, my collies, the love of my life Elaine and all my friends to come about. My friends, and I can't name you all, but you have all been special. The most influential, Jock MacDonald, who has featured from start to finish, Lennie Dodgson, Jimmy O'Donnell, Wattie Nicholson and Bobby Sinton from my younger days and throughout the story. Jim Innes, Jim and Anne Stevenson, Sam Hoatson, Kenny Paton, John McDonald Jr, Hank Duncan, Willie Wightman, Alan Short, Jimmy Culter, Ron Cooper, Billy Hill, Karl Smith and Jeremy and Darren, Martin Haynes, Craig Anderson, Charlie and Kevin Boyd and Ifty and Naz Ahmed, and Brian and Debbie Taylor from the later brigade. Alex Ferguson, Martin Ferguson, Martin Buchan, Dave Mackay, Jack Berry, Bobby Elliott, Mark Johnston and Dandy Nicholls from the famous brigade. My aunts, uncles, cousins, all my Army mates, RSMs and commanding officers. I thank the Lord for lending me you lot for all these years and I hope He can see His way clear to extending my loan for many years to come. Thanks a million all of you.

When I wrote the last chapter of the book, I thought that's it, but almost two years have passed and so much has happened that an epilogue was a must.

First of all, I contacted *The Sun* newspaper, who showed interest but it turned out that what they really wanted was an interview with Alex Ferguson. Alex even phoned me from his holiday in France instructing me to get *The Sun* to contact his son Jason for comments on the book. They still continued to send emails and as a result were kicked into touch.

Next up was the *Daily Record* and I actually took two of their journalists to meet Alex. A journalist is supposed to be able to spot a story, but they could spot Edinburgh Castle from Princes Street. Needless to say, I haven't bought a copy of the paper since.

Finally things came right when I contacted the *Daily Star* and was put in touch with, Ben Boreman, and editor with the *Daily Express*. He has been superb in helping me edit and typeset the book, and if it were down to me he'd win Journalist of the Year, hands down. Ben contacted JMD Media and their managing director Steve Caron, who was impressed and, subject to approval from his editor Michelle Grainger, reckoned we had a winner. Michelle gave the green light so we are going to print. Whether it is going to go anywhere now is up to you, the punters, but I am eternally grateful to Ben, Steve and Michelle for their faith in me. Thank you all.

Other events that have occurred in the interim are as follows:

We were at Haydock for our annual outing 18 months ago, Alex Ferguson had a runner, Red Force One, trained by Tom Hascombe and ridden by Richard Kingscole (a superb trainer-jockey combination it must be said) and he let us have his badges on the horse. I went over to Tom during the meeting to thank him and was introduced to one of his owners, Caroline Ingram.

Caroline's horse Teodoro won the last race and we won a right few bob. We became friends and I took Caroline, her father Bob and son James to Old Trafford and Caroline invited me up to Michael Owen's suite at Chester Races. Caroline has another horse, a colt called Jackstar who has a big future and may well have won the 2,000 Gns before this goes to print. Caroline was awarded an OBE for her generous charity work – she is one class lady, honest as the day is long, and it's a pleasure to have her as a friend and to be considered a friend of hers.

At the same time at Old Trafford I met an Irish family, Michael and Pauline Griffin and their children Charlie and Micheala, and we have become the closest of friends. Michael and Charlie came over to Blackpool and we went to the Manchester United v Everton game, where we met up with Caroline and her family and a close friend of Alex's, Pete Joyce. I have become close friends with Pete and his wife Jo, another lovely lady.

I took Pete and Damien Hilton to Haydock and Jo did all the driving, allowing us to partake in consuming the demon drink.

Michael and Pauline invited me over to their home in Ballybofey, County Donegal, and it was the most relaxing three days I have had since I lost my collie Jock. Michael took me to his local, Heeneys, where mine host Eugene and his punters gave me a great Irish welcome. The craic was brilliant and if you ever go across the sea to Ireland try and visit Ballybofey and Heeneys.

Another Irishman to come on the scene was Peirce Penney, and we have become great friends and regularly exchange racing information.

So, there again you have it, as I've mentioned before, the Irish and Glaswegians are the salt of the earth.

That's all the good news now unfortunately. After a battle against illness, we lost Sandy Nicholls – a sad day for racing. His record of six Ayr Gold Cups and every other major sprint will never be beaten.

Right after that, my lifelong friend John MacDonald passed away. They say these things come in threes and when the news broke that Alex Ferguson had suffered a life-threatening collapse I though please God no.

Thankfully everyone's prayers were answered and Alex pulled through. His wife Cathy is staunch in her faith. My mother always taught me to have faith so never be ashamed to admit to having faith in your God. Faith pulled Alex through and everyone who prayed for his recovery has had that faith win the day.

That's about it. When the book goes to print I hope everyone who buys it enjoys reading it as much as I enjoyed writing it. It's just sad that the two men who inspired me most to write it, Davy Mackay and Jack MacDonald are no longer with us, but you will never be forgotten. Thanks a million for all the memories.

ND - #0099 - 270225 - C0 - 234/156/11 - PB - 9781780915968 - Gloss Lamination